UPRISING IN THE CITY

Made in America

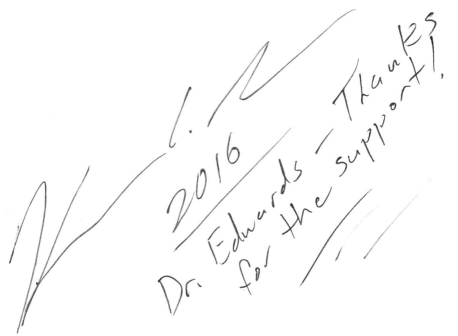

2016
Dr. Edwards — Thanks
for the support!

KEVIN SHIRD

Author of 'Lessons of Redemption'

Uprising in the City
©2016 Kevin Shird

ISBN: 978-1-68419-504-6

Cover Photography: Joe Giordano

Printed in the United States of America

I'm the biggest hypocrite of 2015

Once I finish this, witnesses will convey just what I mean

I mean, it's evident that I'm irrelevant to society

That's what you're telling me, penitentiary would only hire me...

~ KENDRICK LAMAR~

I know I got it made while the masses of black people are catchin' hell, but as long as they ain't free, I ain't free!

~MUHAMMAD ALI~

CONTENTS

FOREWORD

by Sheri Booker

When Freddie Gray died, the people of Baltimore were outraged. Everyone wanted to know how another young black man could lose his life while in police custody. And when the answers were unclear, frustration and anger spilled over into the streets. There was an *Uprising in the City* as some citizens literally set Baltimore on fire. In his book, Kevin Shird narrates the story of how this all transpired, but he has also mapped out a plan to make sure it never happens again.

It's difficult to ignore the many ills that plague Baltimore and several other urban cities around the United States. But it is clear that now is the time for change. In this brilliantly bold book, Kevin takes the lead on addressing how to solve some of these problems on every level, from education to government to community service. He isn't afraid to confront the difficult topics head-on in a loving but firm way. Voices are important but it is actions that truly invoke change. And this book convinces you to get outside of yourself, take a chance and become a part of the revolution.

I still remember the first time I heard Kevin speak about his personal journey. He was in Atlanta being honored for his first book, *Lessons of Redemption*. In a room filled with hundreds of strangers, he opened up about what it's like to grow up in the inner city, being lured into the drug game, serving over a decade in prison, and then being released to become a youth advocate. Despite his path, one thing was clear, Kevin was a proud son of Baltimore—and he still is today. If anyone knows anything about redemption and transformation, it's this author. It's because of his unique perspective that he is able to take a tragedy and find triumph. Baltimore deserves to have its story told by someone who understands it. And Freddie Gray deserves to have his memory honored by someone who understands and has compassion for the streets.

At times the pages of *Uprising in the City* reads like a firer history book, carefully providing the background of a city deeply segregated, in need of police and education reform. But instead of placing blame or judgment, this book provides some concrete solutions to moving forward.

I have read many think pieces and articles about the city I was born and raised in. I have watched many debates and discussions on the issue. But *Uprising in the City* is the cheat sheet to true reform and redemption for a great city with the potential to become even greater. With all of the commentary about the aftermath of the unrest, Kevin Shird is providing the blueprint to help rebuild a city that could have burned to the ground. *Uprising in the City* is a book that needed to be written and only Shird could tell the story of Baltimore with this much precision and accuracy. Filled with compassion and unadulterated truth this book is the key to transforming a troubled city into the beautiful metropolis that it can be.

INTRODUCTION

A City in Turmoil

The car was ablaze and the flames were roaring ten feet into the air near the corner of North and Fulton Avenues in Baltimore on April 27, 2015. The unrest was spiraling out of control—rioters set property on fire to show their displeasure. One could easily imagine this in Afghanistan or Iraq, where religious extremists fought to control the streets and decimate the opposition. But this was not Afghanistan or Iraq; this was a street corner in a major American city when the motherland should have been tranquil. As the melee with police continued, cars and buildings burned in pockets throughout the city. The violence was real, and Armageddon was standing at the border, waiting to enter.

The citizens weren't completely shocked at the mayhem that exploded in the streets. The conditions that led to the uprising had been developing for decades—and the government knew it. The Freddie Gray police brutality case was the match that ignited the fuel of poverty, unemployment, urban decay, inequality, and racial injustice. Now the world was watching the rioting and looting escalate across Baltimore. As the fear spread, violence and crime were unleashed, the taming of this giant was, at the moment, impossible.

America was stunned. Cable news anchors and pundits described the scene of torched property and businesses in live broadcasts to the shocked world. The infamous burning of the CVS Pharmacy store on the corner of Pennsylvania and North Avenue played in a loop. Many viewers couldn't believe their eyes, as a US city came under siege on live television. It was the best reality show around, and yes, it was real.

Within hours, news outlets across the world raced to Baltimore, a city known more for delicious crabs, but these journalists weren't after seafood. They wanted the big story, the one on the sea of protests that engulfed Baltimore. And why? What was it about this particular case—Freddie Gray's death—that sparked fury across the city?

The booming sound of the protesters was like an echo from a twelve-gauge shotgun blast, as the chants of "All night, all day, we gonna fight for Freddie Gray" and "What do we want? Justice! When do we want it? Now!" reverberated through the streets. From Sandtown-Winchester to East Monument Street, emotions were raw.

I was there, walking through the streets of my hometown, feeling the energy that spread through the concrete jungle. I thought to myself, "This is as real as it gets."

As I traveled up Pennsylvania Avenue, in the distance I could see my friend, the "Warrior Lawyer" educating the demonstrators on Civil Rights 101. A little farther down the block, at North Avenue, I could see dozens of young brothers, like Dayvon Love, making their presence known. There were no signs of the infamous "Diamond in the Raw" crew pushing heroin in the streets. Those days were long gone. And the dope boys from the East side to the West side had temporarily traded in their Glocks and other handguns for posters reading: JUSTICE FOR FREDDIE GRAY.

As I approached the Enoch Pratt Library near the corner of Pennsylvania Avenue, I saw young people from my city glued to the words "Black Lives Matter" and eager to see changes in policing policies. There were brothers who I knew were fresh out of the penitentiary, caught up in the middle of the action, though they had little choice in the matter. Close to the front of the pack, I could see my activist friend Tenne wearing her DON'T SHOOT T-shirt, rallying the streets. The drama was real.

It was a collage of black, white, and Hispanic bodies moving shoulder to shoulder through the maze, protesting indifference and injustice. Through their tears and their fears, young men, women, and children joined together to give voice to an emotion—an emotion that had long been ignored in Baltimore and throughout the nation. There had previously been a paralysis in the city. The downtrodden were held hostage by poverty. But in this moment in time, which will linger forever, the anger of the underserved and the marginalized boiled over and gave witness to a new world order. And the nation took notice. They noticed not only what happened in Baltimore, but they noticed the same anger felt in dispossessed communities in other cities. It was another wake-up call that reverberated through the minds of the status quo.

While the world observed and debated what happened and why, the citizens had their own perspective on the matter, perspectives that had been smoldering for decades. Everyone—from the eight-year-old boy on the East side who wondered why his elementary school was closed to the seventy-five-year-old retired business owner who survived the 1968 Baltimore riots—was experiencing the nightmare. Everyone had an opinion about whose fault it was.

The Inspiration for *Uprising in the City*

My proximity to these protests for justice was the catalysts for writing this book. The upheaval in an urban metropolis fighting with its past and present—a city engulfed by the heat of the moment and its own smoldering history. What began on April 12 and in the days that followed was a turning point in the history of the city. Before it was over, a narrative was created about what went wrong to fuel this conflagration in a major American city that, on the surface, seemed to be a place of urbanity and charm.

While this book is focused on what happened in Baltimore, it can provide a lens through which to look at other cities experiencing some of the same issues. The split in society between the haves and have-nots has taken on a racial cast. The vast majority of the urban poor in Baltimore, as in most major cities, are African-Americans. By all social measures, African-Americans as a group have suffered much more than their white counterparts because of lower incomes, poorer housing, and worse health and shorter life expectancy. Many feel excluded from the vision of the United States as a melting pot where all have access to the Dream. But many do not, hence the anger erupting not just in Baltimore, but in cities across the nation. The rage against injustice is released by an inciting incident, like the cry of "police misconduct" fueling many of these clashes.

One of my reasons for writing *Uprising in the City* is to draw attention to the truth and to discuss possible solutions. What changes should be implemented to move the city forward? And who can make these changes happen? Since the infamous uprising of 2015, the city has become the blueprint for change, in part because legislators and mayors watching from around the nation see Baltimore as an example of what not to do. Not only did the rioting tap into a reservoir of anger over living conditions and injustice, but some fault was found with the way the government battled internally over how to respond to the eruption. It is very possible that the action or inaction of the police and National Guard in the city may have contributed to the conflagration.

The presence of the National Guard, with their weapons, didn't calm the city down by thwarting violence. Their presence cast a cloud on the city and triggered resistance behind the scenes. Charm City had become an occupied zone.

What's in the Book

This book may not be politically correct and may offend my political connections. But the truth is more powerful than any Facebook post, tweet, or rock that can be thrown in one's direction. My motive is pure and my conscience is clear. *Uprising in the City* explores the unrest from different perspectives. I bring to this story my point of view from my observations, experiences, and feelings, as an author and a National Youth Advocate dedicated to helping inner city youth understand and escape the perils of street culture. The book also includes interviews with key people in Baltimore.

The book also discusses breaking the cycle of problems that have plagued Baltimore for decades. It suggests solutions on how to relieve poverty and unemployment in a city where jobs have poured out for years. Baltimore is a former industrialized municipality, and the globalization has ripped out its nucleus, leaving it searching for a new identity. The book explores some painful truths about poverty intended to show its side effects.

We dive into some realities that on the surface seem rational… until the truth is revealed. For example, a minimum-wage job in a McDonald's restaurant won't lift a person out of poverty, but a college education will. With the incarceration rate in Baltimore and throughout America among the highest in the world, the book asks some hard questions. Among them: How do we ensure that formerly incarcerated men and women become part of the solution? How can we convince corporate moguls from Nike, Under Armour, and Apple to build and assemble more products here in America—and why not in Baltimore?—as part of a job creation strategy? How do we convince corporate America that exercising their corporate responsibility to create jobs in American cities is more desperately needed now than ever?

Lastly, *Uprising in the City* looks at other urban cities across the country, and their connections and similarities in facing the same issues that Baltimore struggles with. The book provides real answers as to how we in Baltimore can become champions of change and set a precedent for the nation to follow.

CHAPTER 1
GRAY SKIES

The feeling in the air was gloomy in the days before the infamous 2015 uprising in Baltimore, Maryland. The tension was thick and emotions were raw. Freddie Gray had died on Sunday, April 19, from injuries he received while in the custody of the Baltimore City police following his arrest on the morning of Sunday, April 12. As the news spread across the city, nerves were uneasy and people were watching closely.

It started as a normal day for me in the place I was born and had lived in my whole life. I know the city and the people well. As an author I spend much of my time these days on conference calls with publishers and agents, discussing manuscripts and speaking engagement opportunities. But somewhere around noon on April 20, I received a text message from a city government official that read in part: "Can you come to city hall for an emergency meeting about Freddie Gray?" This meeting would be hosted by Mayor Stephanie Rawlings-Blake and Police Commissioner Anthony Batts. Of course they wanted a meeting, Freddie Gray was the most pressing issue in the city.

The community was stressed, looking for answers to what happen to the young man who died from a partially severed spinal cord. Shortly before 2:00 p.m., I arrived for the meeting at city hall. The conference room was occupied by about twelve community organizers, activists, and pastors from some of the most prominent churches in the city. Most of the people in the room had worked in the community for years and were well respected in the streets. As I walked through the heavy wooden door, the Baltimore City Director of Community Engagement, Gus Augustus, was also in attendance. His department was a division of the mayor's office and I had known him for years. Our friendship went all the way back to middle school and through our younger days running around the streets. We reconnected during his years of working with former mayor and governor, Martin O'Malley. After some pleasantries—"Kevin, how you doing man?" "Thanks for coming brother."—he said, "You OK man?"

I said: "Absolutely! When are we getting started?"

"The mayor should be here in a second."

As we waited, I introduced myself to others in the room, including the Reverend Frank Reid, a pillar of the community from Bethel A.M.E. Church in West Baltimore. He had been on the front lines in Baltimore and Chicago for decades helping people in tough situations work through their issues. He was committed to the cause of saving lives and he knew the streets.

The Meeting

As Mayor Rawlings-Blake walked into the room and greeted her guests, she seemed calm and relaxed, but many of us were anxious to talk. Some were still wondering why they were called here.

As the mayor spoke, I began to understand the importance of this gathering. It was more detailed information about the police brutality case of Freddie Gray, as implied in the unexpected text message I had received. The mayor started with an update about the death of the young man the day before he died at Johns Hopkins Hospital. She briefly described the city's commitment to fully investigating the death. Then the police commissioner spoke for a moment before introducing his deputy commissioner, who was sitting to my left at the large conference table. The deputy seemed to be a mild-mannered gentleman. We had actually met very briefly a few times at some community events in the city over the years, but nothing beyond that.

The deputy commissioner had a manila folder sitting on the table in front of him, which seemed customary for any meeting, so it didn't set off any alarm bells. As he spoke he slowly opened the folder. I noticed that his hand was shaking slightly. Despite my many meetings with prominent officials, all my speaking engagements across the country, even my visits to the White House, in many ways I'm still a guy from the streets of West Baltimore. So I'm still in the habit of closely observing body language. Back when I was a hustler on the streets, you had to always watch a guy's body language. Forget what he's actually saying, you always had to watch his eyes and pay attention to his hands. It could mean the difference between life and death.

He opened up the manila folder. Slowly, he removed a picture from the folder—the knife Freddie Gray was carrying when he was arrested by police on April 12.

Right away I was dismayed. I understood why he showed us the picture of the knife. He said, "As you all may have heard, there is a dispute regarding the knife Mr. Gray was carrying on the day of his arrest. We want to put that dispute to rest today with some facts about the case."

I thought, "Now the fix is in." I knew police misconduct existed because I had witnessed it up close and personal, but this was different, this was another level. This was the kind of government manipulation you only see in movies.

Then, while the deputy commissioner held the picture of the knife, Commissioner Batts chimed in. He talked about state law and the requirements to possess such a weapon in terms of the length of its blade. "The knife Freddie Gray was carrying was illegal, point blank, and that's our position, meaning that the arrest by my officers was justified."

I understood why we were there. We were supposed to provide some kind of citizen's cover for the city's position. We were invited there to become surrogates for the city's cause. We were supposed to return to our communities, to our neighborhoods and tell everyone what we had just learned from authorities. We had been recruited by Baltimore's city government to send a message to the world that Freddie Gray was a thug carrying an illegal weapon, and his arrest was legitimate.

As the conversation continued, I realized that this move wasn't the type of misconduct I had assumed it would be, like a bag of money passed underneath the table containing a million dollars in unmarked bills. This was designed to keep the peace and calm the people in the streets. This was a preemptive strike on the critics.

Yes, something needed to be done to quell the rising tide of tension in the city, triggered by Freddie Gray's death. But was this the right way? The media was going wild. They wanted answers. Jane Miller from *WBAL News* was hot on the heels of the administration and the police department. Everyone in the local media smelled blood in the water. The debate over what really happened went back and forth and was more tense by the day. So the city leaders wanted to present this claim about the knife because if the knife was within the parameters allowed by law, then Gray's arrest would have been unwarranted.

From what I gathered looking at the photo, it seemed like an average pocket knife—nothing menacing. Attending this meeting was so surreal, like I had been inserted into a clandestine story of espionage, a room full of bystanders used like pawns in a game of chess.

As the meeting continued and I absorbed the information presented, I was getting frustrated. I struggled to stay professional and not vent. If the knife could be classified as an illegal weapon, the department could justify the arrest. They could say it was a "clean arrest." On the other hand, if the knife Freddie Gray was carrying was legal to possess under Maryland state law, he should never have been arrested and loaded in the back of that police transport at all. He shouldn't have been there at all and he should be alive today.

The text message, the "emergency meeting" notice, the focus of the meeting really was to persuade "us" that Freddy Gray's arrest was valid. And there was something else I realized. Throughout the conversation there was one big piece of the puzzle that we never discussed: the treatment of Freddie Gray in the back of the police transport. How did he sustain the spinal injuries that killed him?

Following the awkward and uncomfortable presentation, time was allotted for a short Q&A. The community organizers and pastors posed questions to our hosts, but most of them were never directly answered. And based on the partial answers they provided, it was my impression that the police department didn't want to give us too much information. They were only willing to scratch the surface.

"I have a question," an elderly woman said. "How do these things keep on happening in the city? The people in our neighborhood are tired and something has to be done about police hurting people. I'm really concerned, and a lot of people are." She continued, "This type of stuff has been going on for too long, mayor. Something has to change soon."

The woman was referring to the long history of police brutality in Baltimore and she was upset. She was well aware of the issues and she was well aware that something should have been done to stop it long ago.

The mayor tried to allay her concern: "I can honestly say that we're working tirelessly along with the police department to address these issues, issues of misconduct, and complaints in the community. We clearly understand that we need a true partnership with the community if we are ever going to make a sustainable impact on crime in Baltimore. I want to work with the community and not against the community."

The woman seemed unconvinced.

A few others in the room shared their opinions with the mayor and Commissioner Batts. They described the tension in the streets behind this situation. As I listened, I thought that this was an eerie conversation and that the entire event seemed so strange.

After the meeting was adjourned, the mood was somber, like there was a cloud over the room. Some in the group whispered among themselves, trying to wrap their heads around the last sixty minutes. The mayor thanked everyone for coming out before rushing off to another engagement. Her mood was mildly upbeat, although her plate was without a doubt very full. As we all walked to the elevators, we had more questions than answers. To most of us, the meeting felt like an awkward exchange. There was a tension looming over the city that couldn't be explained.

On the elevator, Gus, Pastor Reid, Pastor Yeary from Douglas Memorial Community Church, and I discussed not just what happened, but the environment in the street.

We exited the elevator and walked across the shiny marble floors toward the front door of city hall. I was looking at all the history on the walls. I was reminded of the historic nature of this building and all the laws and ordinances enacted by politicians in Baltimore for over a century. Did they ever before face these types of issues, I wondered?

As the air cooled and early evening approached, we stood outside city hall for another thirty minutes, talking about next steps—what should we do? What could we do now? We talked about making sure that we continued a dialogue with the community. They had a right to know what was going on. The people were frustrated because the city officials were telling them to trust the process, that the case was under investigation. But many residents were saying to themselves, "We've trusted you in the past and never saw any results."

Sensing the Tension

As I drove home, my head was pounding from thinking too hard. I tried to gauge the temperature of the people on the streets. I was looking for signs of tension, signs of uneasiness about the situation. It's not something you can describe, it's just a feeling you get when you know something just isn't right. It's the little voice inside that's trying to tell you something, but you can't quite put your finger on what it is.

Driving through downtown, it seemed I could sense people were upset about the death of Freddie. The writing was on the proverbial wall. I wondered what was going on in the rest of the city, in the places where emotions run deep. How are those people reacting to the situation? I wondered. What are they feeling? What's the real vibe in the city, where the opinions of the people living in poverty rarely count?

Craving answers, I drove directly up Fayette Street toward the west side. I needed to go back to the old neighborhood first. I had to make sure I wasn't underestimating or even overestimating this situation. I needed to make sure I was on the same page with the people. On Fayette Street, it seemed like I stopped at every red light in my path. It's only about two miles from downtown, but it felt like ten. Finally making it to South Mount Street, I pulled over to the corner for a second and stared at the ravaged neighborhood. I looked out at the old houses and places where we used to hustle dime bags of heroin many years before, and the memories were vivid.

As I drove, I was reminded of what poverty and the pain of marginalized people looks like. I had been away, speaking around the country to youth about staying away from drugs and abusive situations. But this was my reawakening, seeing people out here who know a lot about police brutality in the streets. These situations have been going on in the Western District of Baltimore for years. The only thing that's new is the creation of the cell phone camera, which turned the heat up on law enforcement officials. Capturing police misconduct on video changed everything. And the video of Freddie Gray dragged off in handcuffs was the initial event that got the people's temperature up—not just for the residents living in poverty in Baltimore, but all across the nation.

Mount Street was mild on this cool early evening and it was a ghost town. I remember hanging out on these same corners with guys who wanted to be superstars, though they didn't have a college education and in many cases, didn't have a high school degree. But while they used to have a dream for themselves, now many were just trying to survive. Making money hustling in the streets was their way to eat, feed their families, and live.

As I drove up Mount Street past the Wally Funeral Home, I thought about all the dead who passed through this undertaker's establishment. Many were elderly residents and people from the block who died prematurely from drugs and murder—all the things we hope we'll never succumb to.

As I got closer to the infamous Western District Police Station, I could see the temperature on the streets had changed. More people were out but it was still mostly calm. It was just another poverty stricken Baltimore neighborhood inside this complicated maze of death. I could see the police moving back and forth from the station house, probably changing shifts. Today they were just human beings with jobs, trying to eat, take care of themselves and their families, and survive—same as the local impoverished residents.

I also thought about how close the Western District was to all the illegal activity in the streets. I used to wonder how anyone could be comfortable selling dope this close to the police station. But now I realized that they probably weren't comfortable at all. They were probably just doing what they needed to survive and put food on their table.

Then, as I observed the block, I wondered: How did we get here, where it was now us against them, the cops against the people of color in the streets? The conflict had been brewing for years in the Western District. It didn't manifest overnight or during Mayor Rawlings-Blake's administration. The anger of the residents also didn't start with Freddie Gray's death. This situation started years ago, when people in poverty were just trying to live and get out. There was little they could do, since they faced a lack of opportunity, high unemployment, and widespread substance abuse.

As I continued up Mount Street toward North Avenue, I realized I was close to the corner of Presbury Street, where Freddie Gray was arrested. This was a tough neighborhood dating all the way back to when streetcars rolled up and down West Baltimore. Now it was even tougher, much of the neighborhood was dominated by the low-income housing Gilmor Homes, drugs, death, and despair.

Like many in Baltimore, Freddie Gray had made it through much of his life in this area the hard way. He had to, since people here struggle with their pain and are lucky to be alive. Freddie was lucky up until that infamous Sunday morning, April 12, when he was chased down by a couple of bicycle cops and arrested—cops who had no idea that they would soon change Baltimore and the national narrative of police brutality.

As I made a right turn in my car from Mount onto North Avenue, I moved closer to Pennsylvania Avenue, which hadn't changed much over the years. It was still a busy place, with lots of people walking the streets. When I arrived at the corner after passing the bus stop full of Baltimoreans, I pulled over to check an email on my iPhone, when suddenly I heard someone yelling.

"Yo, Kev, what's up?"

I was startled for a second until I realized it was a guy named Twin, whom I knew well. He was a guy from the streets and I was surprised to see that he was even still alive. I hadn't seen this guy in ten years or more. Twin was a heroin addict and a stick-up boy who went around robbing people to get cash. We had known each other since my days on the West side streets, and I knew he was a guy to be very careful around. He had a quick temper and trigger finger. He was also a killer!

"It's all good, bro," I responded, as I climbed out of my car and onto the busy street corner.

As I walked toward him, Twin said: "I thought I saw you riding past the bus stop, but I wasn't sure if that was you. At first I thought you was a cop with that fucking suit on."

We both laughed.

"Fuck you, man!" I said.

"Naw, man, I'm just bullshitting. I saw you last year on the news and shit talking about kids. You work with kids or something like that, right?

"That's it, bro," I said. "I retired from these streets a long time ago, man. I wrote a book last year about me growing up here in Baltimore and the shit took off. It's called *Lessons in Redemption* and I do a lot of speaking now around the country with young people and shit like that."

"Damn, bro, that's what's up!" Twin stated. "You been doing that shit for a whole year?"

"About eighteen or nineteen months now with the book. But I been working with kids for about six years. I do a lot of work around drug prevention, stuff like that."

"I ain't seen you since that day at Lexington Market, remember? You were just coming home from the penitentiary. Shit, that was back in, what, 2006?"

"Damn, that was oh-six. Time is flying, bro! You right! I had just got out of prison,"

Twin went on to say, "Man, I thought you was going back to running shit when I saw you in oh-six. Back to selling dope on Fayette and Mount Street. Your crew was making crazy money back in the day."

But that was back then, Twin was reminiscing about a time in my life that was long gone. But many guys hold onto the past, because the past is all they have.

"Naw, bro! I had to get away from that shit," I replied. "I couldn't spend the rest of my life in prison. But what about you? What you up to these days?"

Twin paused for a second, "Man, I'm out here doing what I gotta do to survive. I gotta eat!"

I could see in his eyes that he was serious and that he was struggling. Life had been tough on him and he was just trying to stay alive.

I continued, asking, "What's going on in the streets these days, bro? What's going on since this Freddie Gray situation"?

"Man, those cops beat the shit out of that kid and killed his ass. That was fucked up, man. These motherfuckers in Western District are out of control. You know that shit, Kev, you've been out here in the streets. You know how those motherfuckers get down."

"I remember how it is, bro, I remember!"

"Man, they ain't gonna stop until one of them motherfuckers get fucked up. Then they'll stop that shit," Twin said, his voice rising with anger. "Man, these fucking streets are so fucked up, bro. I don't know who to worry about the most…the niggas I'm hanging out with or the cops!"

Suddenly, I felt like it was time to go. While it was good seeing Twin again, our conversation was a stark reminder that this was no longer my life. So I told Twin, "I need to get out of here now, man. Need to get over to the east side, bro. Stay safe out here, man. I don't want to see you on the evening news. When you're ready to get out of these streets, call me, bro. Take my card."

Twin paused for a second while staring at the card and then exclaimed, "Ain't this some shit. This nigga got business cards now and shit!"

We both laughed, and I told Twin, "Fuck you, man! I'm out of here."

I walked back to my car and continued on my way. It was good seeing Twin again and knowing that some of the guys I knew from the streets were still living and breathing. It was astonishing how resilient a man can be. Twin had been shot up three or four times and in and out of prison since a teenager. He had also been injecting heroin for over twenty years, and somehow he was still walking the streets. Incredible!

As I looked out the car window at the many blocks of Baltimore, I saw people on the corners hustling and bustling, trying to make a dollar out of fifteen cents. I thought about how this was their world. Every day, they faced the good, the bad, and the indifferent, but this is how they lived. When you're from a poverty-stricken neighborhood, living day to day can be tough. You have to figure out how to feed yourself and your kids. You have to ask yourself: "How am I going to pay the next telephone bill?"

When you live here, you may not realize how bad it really is because you don't have a lot to compare it to. You're living in a world restricted by poverty and nothing else matters but surviving. All that single mothers with three or four kids know is this: "My children are hungry and I've got to feed them." Or they think, "My children need clothes, so I've got to do what a mother's got to do to get what they need."

I thought about the fate of a young man of seventeen or eighteen years old who had already been arrested five times and dropped out of school in the ninth grade. I asked myself: "What is his life going to look like when he doesn't have a support system to turn things around? What are the prospects for his future in America?"

People don't understand that most who live in the projects and in poverty were born there. They are not in a situation they asked to be in or want to stay in. They did not say, "I want to be poor for the rest of my life." They weren't millionaires one day and suddenly things fell apart. They didn't have a choice, and so now they're just trying to survive.

Freddie Gray was just trying to survive. Certainly, neither he nor the officers who arrested him that day expected that a simple arrest, much like the hundreds of arrests for minor crimes every day, would lead to his death. But in a matter of days, another black man was dead at the hands of police officers.

It's a picture we've seen before. We saw it in Ferguson with the killing of Michael Brown by a cop. We saw it in Staten Island with Eric Garner, who was choked to death by a police officer when he was arrested for the crime of selling loose cigarettes. The officer put him in a chokehold and pushed his face to the ground, after which Garner repeated, "I can't breathe, I can't breathe," until he lost consciousness.

It's a pattern we've seen for years—the police arresting African-Americans for minor crimes and then roughing us up. Now the community's anger is boiling over. I said to the mayor at our emergency meeting that, in situations like this, it's important to have good relationships with the community, because perception is everything.

For example, in the Western District of Baltimore, there is the perception, and the reality, that when you run from the cops and get caught, you'll get beaten up. When I was in the streets dealing drugs, we knew that if you ran from the police, you better run fast and far, so they don't catch you.

So when Freddie Gray got arrested, the perception in the streets was that he ran, got caught, and got beat. That's why I told the mayor and the police commissioner that it's important to have a good relationship with the community in situations like this, because the community's reaction is based on their perception. Because whether Freddie was beaten up by the police or not, it looks that way to the community, and that's all that matters at the time.

It seemed like the mayor and police commissioner understood and agreed with what I told them, since Mayor Rawlings-Blake nodded her head in agreement, and since many other activists and community leaders have had this conversation with them for a long time about community relationships. In fact, Police Commissioner Batts told me that he had been trying to change the culture to improve police-community relationships and that's why he came to Baltimore. So, I felt like he gets it and understands what needs to be done.

The Week of April 20

For the remainder of the week, I continued writing and working on my youth advocacy work across the city, mostly speaking to the young people in schools. Wherever I went, I spoke with students on how to cope with the stress of what they see every day in the streets. I typically spoke—and still do—about drug prevention and how to deal with an abusive environment, since my goal for years has been to keep young people away from drugs and out of prison. It's a passion I have because of my own mistakes as a kid in Baltimore.

But that week I noticed many of the students wanted to discuss the Freddie Gray case and police brutality in the city. Even young people were concerned about the death of the twenty-five-year-old man in Sandtown-Winchester.

No one could know that things would intensify the way they did across the country. The tension was obvious after Ferguson and Staten Island, but I had no idea that Baltimore would be one of the many cities where similar eruptions made national news. These upheavals were a response to Jim Crow, still alive and well in the inner cities, where people suffered poverty, unemployment, and a growing frustration that things would never change.

A timeline published by the *Baltimore Sun* helps to show how this incident opened a festering sore of anger that turned into the uprising in the city.

In another *Baltimore Sun* article, Justin Fenton and Jessica Anderson described how Police Commissioner Batts, with Mayor Rawlings-Blake standing behind him, held a press conference in which he acknowledged that Freddie Gray had repeatedly asked for medical care, but did not receive it during the arrest that preceded his death. They also pointed out that the police wrote in court documents that Freddie Gray was arrested "without force or incident" for having a switchblade knife, but then "suffered a medical emergency during transport." But while the case sparked outrage, the police said little about what happened, stating the case was under investigation. Presumably, the article noted, Gray was stopped because he "fled unprovoked upon noticing police presence" and that's when "they found a knife clipped to the inside of his front pants pocket and placed him under arrest."

But then, as the article continued, Officer Garrett Miller, who wrote the report, stated that while Gray was transported by police van to the Western District, he had a medical emergency and the van driver immediately took him to the shock trauma unit of the hospital. Yet, as Batts acknowledged at the press conference, Gray repeatedly asked for medical care when he was first arrested. He asked for an inhaler for his asthma, but he did not receive it, because the officer did not have one with him. Batts then acknowledged that the department was "reviewing its policies related to prisoner transports and when officers should call medics for suspects," since there were "many occasions [when] medics should have been called."

Also, the article noted that the police van stopped to put leg irons on Gray and then to pick up another prisoner before taking both to the Western District, where the police called a medic to attend to Gray. But the initial video of the incident, which showed a portion of the arrest, did not show the excessive use of force when Gray was arrested. Also, there was no video of what happened to Gray in the back of the van since the van did not have a camera, so the cause of Freddie Gray's spine injuries was unclear. But whatever happened in the van was very serious, since Gray's family attorney said his spinal cord had been severed, and after surgery at Shock Trauma, he died on April 19, a week after his arrest. Soon after that, the officers involved in his transport were placed on an administrative assignment, pending the outcome of the investigation.

Reading this article and reviewing the timeline, I can better understand why the mayor and police commissioner reached out to us to help reduce the fallout from the incident. They wanted us there to show they had the support of the community when they sought to justify Freddie Gray's arrest by claiming he had an illegal knife. After all, the rest of the story sure looked bad for them—and it would be even worse, since there would have been no basis for his arrest if the knife was legal. The reason everything looked so bad is that Gray hadn't just been beaten up by the police, he had died. Worse, he didn't appear to have run at all, since after he was stopped and the police found the knife, they arrested him "without force or incident," to use the police officers' own words in their report. In other words, Gray didn't try to resist the arrest, and still he died. So, sure, it looked bad for the police, and presumably the mayor and police commissioner called on us to help soothe the growing anger in the community and spread the story that Gray's arrest was legal.

Still, at the time, I thought the intensity would gradually simmer down and the story would fade away, but it didn't.

How the Story Kept Getting Bigger

As the timeline of incidents in the story shows, the situation grew and grew, while I went about my everyday life. I didn't realize how it would trigger the growing rage within Baltimore, not only about police brutality and racial injustice, but about everything else that turned Baltimore into two cities: one of haves and one of increasingly desperate have-nots.

What were these other incidents? Here in brief is what happened in the week before Baltimore exploded.

On April 21, the six officers involved—the three on bikes who arrested Gray and the others—were identified. That afternoon, members of Maryland's Congressional delegation asked the US Department of Justice to open a criminal civil rights investigation. Shortly afterward, a department spokesman announced that they were opening a probe, along with the FBI, US Attorney's Office, and civil rights lawyers in the US Department of Justice, to determine whether any civil rights violations had occurred. Among other things, the investigation was going to look into whether Gray was properly restrained in the van, where his injuries occurred.

So initially, looking back, it seemed like the mayor, police commissioner, and US Justice Department were doing the right thing in looking into the incident. Especially since Tessa Hill-Aston, president of the Baltimore chapter of the NAACP, said that "extra scrutiny from the Justice Department is important" because the police don't have a good record of investigating themselves. The article reported that the Justice Department's

Community Oriented Policing Services Office was already conducting a "collaborative review" of the city's Police Department, including the agency's use-of-force reports and investigations, training procedures and policies. So, on the surface, it appeared that the community of Baltimore was finally being heard.

But the city was still tense. We were into our fourth straight day of protests, this time gathering at the intersection where Gray was arrested. From there, Justin George's article in the *Baltimore Sun*, bore the headline: "Tensions Remain High After Gray's Death." Then protesters marched to the Western District Police Station, where officers had pulled Gray's unresponsive body out of the transport van. Along the way, the crowd "chanted, prayed, and demanded changes." One factor contributing to the anger was that the city had not given the community a thorough explanation as to how Gray was injured. So, the lack of transparency helped to fuel their anger because they believed the mayor and police were hiding something. Then, too, contributing to the protests were the allegations of police brutality and the racial injustice issues that were already a source of national concern.

At the time, though, I still thought of this as a case of another black guy running from the police, getting caught, and getting beat up. Yet the stories in the *Baltimore Sun* showed that there were serious questions about what really happened that the police were answering, and this contributed to the growing anger. For example, Mayor Rawlings-Blake, who had previously been a public defender, noted that there was insufficient information about why Gray was pursued in the first place, because "having a knife is not necessarily probable cause to chase or arrest someone."

Then Billy Murphy, the attorney for Gray's family, highlighted how little information there was when he said that the Police Department's acknowledgement that Gray made multiple requests for medical assistance but did not receive it "is a major issue that affects all residents." Moreover, Murphy pointed out that "running while black is not a crime…Being afraid of police and running from them, in retrospect, is a great idea. He just didn't run fast enough." He also observed that the police delay in providing an explanation for the stop showed that they didn't want to admit liability. As he commented: "If you're still searching for probable cause after the arrest, what does that tell you? They should just fess up."

On the 22, the police announced they had statements from five of the six police officers about what happened, though the mayor wondered why they were missing a statement from one officer. Later that night, the Baltimore police union president made matters worse by comparing the Freddie Gray protests to a "lynch mob," since the protesters called for the officers involved to be jailed immediately. The use of that term only fueled the protests. As Murphy said, he couldn't understand why the Baltimore police union could liken the protesters to a "lynch mob" when the police had a history of lynching black people in America. An odd statement coming from a police union president, but the damage was done. Murphy called on the police for "an immediate apology and a retraction."

But the police's response was neither an apology nor immediate, so the protests continued. Though there may have been fewer people, now the protests were at times more tense, as the marchers chanted, "No justice, no peace," and "All night, all day, we gonna fight for Freddie Gray." Certainly Police Commissioner Batts tried to defuse things by meeting with representatives of the protesters and the Gray family to express his sympathy and updating them on the investigation.

Yet, for all of the local efforts to diffuse the crisis, it was obvious that something more serious was happening. Like many in Baltimore, I was still not fully aware of how things were spiraling out of control. But they were, which is why Governor Larry Hogan said he felt he must send the Maryland State Police to deal with the intensifying protests.

Still, the protests continued to be relatively peaceful on the afternoon and evening of April 23. Though the police arrested a few protesters, nonviolence prevailed while the police and city leaders took new steps to maintain order. Among other things, they canceled leave for officers, so more officers would be on the streets, and they allowed city employees to leave early to reduce traffic congestion.

It's no wonder, in the face of these growing protests, that civil rights groups—including the ACLU and NAACP—called on Governor Hogan to help fix the fractured relationship between Baltimore residents and the police by convening a special session to pass body camera laws and to immediately invest funding into urban renewal projects. They wanted the governor to address some of the broader problems that the Freddie Gray case exposed about poverty, police brutality, and inequality.

Governor Hogan did make some effort to address the problems. He announced that he would sign three bills into law that would encourage police departments to begin body-camera programs and require them to report police-related deaths to the Maryland State Police. He also announced that he would sign legislation to double the amount of money people injured by the police can collect in civil lawsuits. Still, many felt that the Republican Governor should have agreed to do more for the city.

The Baltimore police tried to make some fixes too, since Commissioner Batts acknowledged that Gray was not buckled into the van as he should have been and that the police who arrested and transported him repeatedly failed to get him medical attention in a timely manner.

Yet, it seemed as if those efforts were too little, too late, since on April 25, during a day of continued protests, some of the protestors turned to violence. They trashed cars and local businesses. They were increasingly angry and frustrated. One witness, who videotaped part of the Freddie Gray arrest on his cell phone, said the police intimidated him after officials called on community members for help in the investigation, and the police released a photo of him as a witness to the arrest. He said he believed the police had released his photo to intimidate him. Even the plea of Freddie's twin sister as she stood by Mayor Rawlings-Blake's side at a news conference on April 26 couldn't calm the growing tension. Though she pleaded, "Please stop the violence," and said her brother would not have wanted it this way.

Later that day, Gray's family held a wake for him at the Vaughn Green East Funeral Home, which drew hundreds of people who either knew him or were moved by his tragic death. The following day, on the 27, the family held a funeral at the prominent New Shiloh Baptist Church on North Monroe Street that drew family, friends, community members, and strangers from all across the city. Since I didn't know Gray personally and was still just an observer at the time, I didn't attend the wake or the funeral.

Much of April 27 was a blur. I felt sick, dealing with a bad cold. I took medication, which caused me to feel like I was in a fog the entire day. After taking more cold meds, I went to bed extremely early not realizing that what was happening would change the face of Baltimore forever. Not only would it change my city, but it put the nation on notice. America would receive a cruel message from Baltimore that there was an immediate need to change a society where poverty and pain had become a way of life for a quarter of its people.

CHAPTER 2
CHAOS IN THE CITY

Waking Up to a City in Chaos

It was early Tuesday morning on April 28, when my eyes slowly crept open from a deep sleep. I glanced over at the clock. It was 5:58 a.m., and my mind was telling me "get up," while my body was still motionless. My usual routine around that time was to turn on the morning news to gauge the pulse of the world before starting my day. Hesitantly, I mustered enough strength to click the remote control to power up the television, just as my favorite morning show began.

The first words I heard coming from the host were "Baltimore is on fire." It was MSNBC's *Morning Joe* and the host Joe Scarborough was making this remarkable statement to the world on live television.

My mind stopped as the words "Baltimore on fire" reverberated through my head. Momentarily, I glanced over at my bedroom window, thinking of an escape route. Where are my Nike shoes? I thought. I may need to do some fast running. I should be getting the hell out of here soon. Then I realized that Joe Scarborough's words where metaphorical. I believe he wanted to grab viewers and shape the conversation about Baltimore and the unrest that had shocked the world. The situation had escalated overnight to unanticipated proportions. Things had changed drastically. There were now thousands of people involved in the mayhem, not just hundreds like the day before.

And how did we get here? Well, just the day before, on Monday, April 27, a huge disturbance exploded at Mondawmin Mall in West Baltimore between school students and police officers. According to an article published by *Mother Jones*— "Eyewitnesses: The Baltimore Riots Didn't Start the Way You Think" —after Baltimore police and a crowd of teens clashed near the mall on Monday afternoon, news reports described the violence as a riot triggered by kids who had been itching for a fight all day. But those interviewed for Mother Jones and other media outlets, along with teachers and parents, maintain that the police actions actually inflamed a tense, but stable, situation.

What really happened is this. The funeral of Freddie Gray at a nearby church, that day, had ended a few hours earlier. According to the *Baltimore Sun*, a call to "purge"—referring to the 2013 dystopian film of that name in which all crime is made legal for one night—circulated on social media that morning among school-aged Baltimoreans. The rumored plan, which was not traced to any specific person or group, was to assemble at the Mondawmin Mall at 3:00 p.m. and proceed down Pennsylvania Avenue toward downtown Baltimore. The Baltimore Police Department, which was aware of the "purge" call, prepared for the worst. Shortly before noon, the department issued a statement that it had "received credible information that members of various gangs…have entered into a partnership to 'take-out' law enforcement officers."

When school let out that afternoon, the police were in the area equipped with full riot gear. According to eyewitnesses in the neighborhood, the police stopped buses and forced riders, including many students who were trying to get home, to get off. Cops shut down the local subway stop and blockaded roads near Mondawmin Mall and Frederick Douglass High School across the street. In effect, they corralled the young people in the area. Not a good idea at all!

So, that morning when I woke up and turned on Morning Joe, I had no idea how things had ramped up the night before. Just before I went to sleep I remember the ruckus at the mall on TV. But, still groggy, I thought it was an isolated event and went back to sleep. I remember waking up a few times throughout the evening to get water and I may have glanced at the television again but I was still out of it from the cold medication.

Baltimore had become a cable news headline story and a talking point across the nation in a matter of hours. Every news show across the country was now calling the situation, "The Baltimore Riots."

Initially the unrest erupted across West Baltimore and downtown. As described in the *Baltimore Sun* article, "Riots erupt: Baltimore descends into chaos, violence, looting," roaming gangs of mostly young men clashed with police in the streets. They seriously injured officers, broke into businesses, and looted their stocks.

So as I slept the night away there was an uprising in the city and when I and others woke up across the nation, this was a real wake-up call. For me, the upheavals became a rallying cry to tell Baltimore's story—of how and why the city erupted and what to do to fix the conditions, not only in Baltimore, but in the whole nation.

The City Responds to the Chaos

However, one might characterize it, that morning, as people woke up, they felt uncertain. No one really knew what would happen next. It could have escalated into a citizenry civil war, though fortunately it didn't, for many reasons, including the response of the city government to contain the situation.

One challenge the city faced was that fires seemed to be targeting particular businesses, those viewed as having been taking advantage of people in the community. For example, many fires in the corner stores where owned by Asians, particularly Koreans, and some Hispanics. In any event, the mayor declared an emergency, bringing the National Guard into the city, turning Baltimore into what felt like a police state. Normally, you don't see the military in an urban environment like Baltimore. But ironically some community members felt at ease with the National Guard, thinking they would help calm down the situation.

But did they calm it down? Or make matters worse? Later, I learned that the mayor, police chief, and other officials had some discussions about the wisdom of bringing in the National Guard. Their concern was whether their presence would exacerbate the situation instead of containing it. But they decided to bring them in and to enact a curfew, so that everyone had to be off the streets of Baltimore by 10:00 p.m. If you were caught on the streets past curfew, you were subject to arrest, unless you were going to work. If you were coming home late from work, you were subject to arrest. Nobody wanted to sit in the Baltimore City detention center just because of a curfew violation, so the city streets were empty, for the most part.

Feelings about the curfew were mixed. Some thought it was justified to keep residents safe, but many thought it was unnecessary. I had two opposing views myself. One side of me felt that, as American citizens, people needed their freedom to live and the curfew took that away. But the other side of me knew that innocent people could be harmed if the curfew was not enacted. I definitely didn't want to see the police or the National Guard kill a black person in the streets.

The National Guard and Curfew

After the mayor's call went out, the National Guard was deployed across Baltimore. Guard soldiers were stationed everywhere starting from the CVS pharmacy at North and Pennsylvania Avenue—that was the epicenter of the riots—to hospitals, city hall, police stations, and all across the city. Everywhere you went, you saw them, which made the city feel weird. Many of the people I knew were unhappy about it, but knew it was pretty much out of our control. Many others were angry, they felt that calling up the Guard never had to happen.

Business owners throughout the city were quite upset. They were losing business because of the curfew and the National Guard presence in the city. They also lost business because people in the surrounding counties and states decided the area was unsafe. They did all they could to avoid coming into Baltimore. This affected virtually all businesses, from hotels and gas stations to 7–Eleven's and supermarkets. What made the whole situation especially weird was that during the day, things were somewhat normal. Although we saw military Humvee's driving down the street. But by 9:30 p.m., most of the streets were empty and Baltimore was like a ghost town.

The Decision to Call in the National Guard

Key officials often have different views on how to move forward with a situation. In this case, the governor felt the mayor should have pulled the trigger much faster on bringing the National Guard into the city. But the mayor wanted time to evaluate the situation and not rush into any decision—a position that made a lot of sense to many Baltimore residents, especially those living in the areas where the National Guard would be concentrated.

In any event, bringing the Guard into Baltimore to deal with looting could have contributed to an even more dangerous situation developing, because of military weapons, which have no place in urban America. Their presence has the potential to create a disaster.

Many Baltimoreans agreed that a lot of thought should go into making that type of decision. On the other hand, the governor felt that the mayor should have made the decision much sooner to protect the business community from high losses. In his view, the Guard would have prevented some of the burning cars and storefronts.

But whatever the thinking, fortunately it did not result in any deaths, which was always a possibility. In hindsight, one can always argue for one option or another, but any thoughts would be speculative, because we don't know what would have happened.

The Role of the Media

A lot of the media reports were inaccurate and sensationalized the story of what was going on in the city. They blew up the pervasiveness of the rioting and the extent of the damage to far more than it was, contributing to the image of "Baltimore on fire." After all, a hyped up story might seem better to them than the real one—and many Americans were sucked right in.

The inaccuracy was not so much about the Freddie Gray story—whether the police treated him appropriately or not, based on people's attitude toward the law and whether they supported the cops or Freddie Gray. Rather, the media was wrong in its coverage of how much burning and looting went on in the city. They presented Baltimore as a city completely on fire, under siege.

In short, the media built the upheavals in Baltimore into a much different story than it was. And such media exaggeration can contribute to the chaos and violence. What CNN in particular did not focus on was the fact that most protesters marched down the streets of Baltimore peacefully. The protesters and the rioters and looters were totally different animals. But the reporting from CNN and some of the other cable and news outlets made them all look like looters and the rioters. The rarely acknowledged the peaceful demonstrators who were in total disagreement with how the police handled the Freddie Gray case.

Reflecting On the Start of the Incident at the Mall

Looking back at that fateful day on April 27 when Mondawmin Mall erupted, consider that that situation never had to happen in the first place. Police essentially corralled hundreds of students together who were trying to get home because the police thought that was the way to control the situation. But by herding everyone in, they created the exact conditions they were trying to avoid.

I discovered much of this after reading a *Baltimore Eclipse* article, "The Battle of Mondawmin,"[1] posted a few days after dwellings around the city began burning. Much of what I read was corroborated by the parents of students who were at the mall that day. I actually knew a few of the parents who were outraged over the situation.

As the article describes, "most of the injuries, arrests, looting, arson, and property destruction" occurred on the night of Monday, April 27, after the confrontation between the heavily armed police and school-age children that began at the Mondawmin Mall.

According to the article, that event should be considered a critical moment in the unfolding of the riots because it was the beginning of an organized police action and it was linked to the "wave of mayhem," which moved into other parts of the city until after midnight.

As the article describes, the way the police mishandled the mall altercation sparked the subsequent riots. Yes, plenty of anger was already building up in Baltimore over the Freddie Gray case, the cycle of poverty, and deteriorating social conditions. But this flare up at the mall severely agitated the public. It was literally the last straw.

Closing the mall early may have been a wise move on the part of the police. But then the police made what I think was a major strategic mistake when they stopped buses and forced riders off, and, even worse, shut down the subway station and blockaded the roads. As the article described it, the result was that the cops "corralled young people in the area…They did not allow the afterschool crowd to disperse." While many parents had picked up their kids from school earlier that day because of their concerns about the rumors, other kids who tried to get home on their own couldn't. They were blocked by the heavily armed cops. And this area is one of the busiest transit hubs in the city and the place hundreds of students use to travel to and from school.

Ironically, no protest activities were scheduled that day because this was the day of Freddie Gray's funeral. But then the mall became the scene of the biggest chaos in the city following Freddie's death. And it was a chaos that very likely would not have happened if the police hadn't corralled the young kids in the mall parking lot. When the first journalists arrived on the scene, they found the students already trapped, with no way out. It seems crazy reading now about how the police trapped the students, but that's what they did, escalating the situation. Meanwhile, the corralled students weren't committing any crimes. In fact, many had their hands raised continually in the air, as if to tell the cops: "Don't shoot, I'm not threatening you." Yet, as many photos and videos of the scene show, the police were treating these young people like enemies of the state.

Then, it would seem, the police actions drove the students to strike back. For example, after they had blocked the students from getting onto the buses, the police assembled in a triangle formation and plunged into the crowd to seize one rowdy student. A photo shows the police pressing the detained students up against the bus stop and grabbing him by the neck, as he objects to being taken in this way. A moment later, the police pull him to the ground and he disappears behind the blue uniforms.

This incident seems to mark a turning point. Soon after, the police advanced across Liberty Heights Avenue, where they confronted people taking shelter on the porches of the homes and some students began throwing things at the police.

"So, why did the army of police cross the road?" the article asks, using photos and videos to illustrate what the police did. Was it to "antagonize civilians on the other side?" I'm not sure, but this action helped to spread the battle to people standing on their property, who had previously been distant observers. But now the police seemed to be calling them to engage. As the article describes: "The police drove armored vehicles directly at people congregated in the Midas parking lot across the street. Anyone in the area was dragged into the conflict." And that included at least one student who got shot with a rubber bullet while just walking down the street.

About this time the police also began to toss missiles back at the students who had been throwing debris, whereupon the students advanced en masse toward the police, who then retreated, in spite of their numbers.

Meanwhile, over the following hours, the situation deteriorated. Crowds grew elsewhere, most notably Pennsylvania and North Avenue, where that CVS was looted and burned, and a check-cashing store was broken into. Meanwhile, the police just stood by and let the looting occur, which was strangely unlike their forceful actions against the students at the mall, who had committed no crime.

After that, the rioting and looting in the city moved south and east, and eventually spread to the downtown area, where police with helmets and shields were stationed at the Lexington Market, the Inner Harbor, and elsewhere. Within a short time, Maryland state troopers arrived to supplement the Baltimore police force. And later, there was looting at the Mondawmin Mall, now undefended since the police had moved their attention to other neighborhoods of the city.

Eventually, over two hundred people were arrested across Baltimore and packed in the jail like sardines, though later most were not charged with any crimes.

Seeing how the mall was the genesis of the rioting that spread throughout the city was amazing. All I could think of was how different the outcome might have been if the students could have gone home. How different things might have been if the police hadn't spread out across the street and drawn in people sitting on their porches. Maybe things would not have gotten out of control if the police hadn't initiated the arrests that led to debris throwing, leading to further police efforts to detain the students. For me, there were many could-have-been scenarios.

After all, in this day of social media journalism and Facebook, people across Baltimore became aware of what was going on at the Mondawmin Mall instantly, fueling the anger of people in other parts of the city, causing reactions.

So, what if the police department had made different decisions on April 27? In hindsight, it's easy now to see all of the mistakes, but it's hard to know what might have happened if the situation at Mondawmin Mall hadn't happened. Maybe that could have changed everything. But then again, maybe not.

Reflections on the Battle over Sending in the National Guard

Besides reflecting on what was and might have been on that fateful night of April 27, I thought about the battle between Mayor Rawlings and Governor Hogan on whether and when to send in the National Guard. The mayor wanted to delay and the governor didn't, and I wondered whether that could have made a difference in what happened next. What the mayor said about how the demonstrators should have the space to destroy things, while probably a slip of the tongue, didn't help matters either.

The controversy escalated at a press conference held Monday night around 9:00 p.m., when Governor Hogan announced that Baltimore Mayor Stephanie Rawlings-Blake had "finally" requested that the National Guard be sent in, as police and citizens "clashed in parts of the city over the arrest and fatal injury of Freddie Gray."[2] When questioned why it took so long for the Guard to arrive, given the violent scenes in the afternoon, Hogan explained that it took him no more than thirty seconds to "declare a national emergency and activate the National Guard," once the mayor called for assistance. Quickly, the governor signed the executive order and the entire team was prepared to leave upon receiving the mayor's request.

But his office had tried to reach the mayor for some time, since he wanted to send in the Guard much sooner, though he had to wait for the mayor's call. The Governor had even wanted to send in the Guard as early as Saturday, when much of the protesting and demonstrating began to become larger and more heated. But Rawlings-Blake stated that she had hesitated, because she didn't want to over-militarize the city's response to the daily protests that started after Freddie Gray death on April 19.[3] She said that in other parts of the country, public officials had made mistakes when they decided "to over-militarize and to bring excessive response to a situation." But once the situation in Baltimore turned from "teenagers to more violence and looting," she then decided to call in the Guard.

Rawlings-Blake defended her decision to wait on the grounds that she had been tested during the city's previous emergencies. She also pointed out that the governor was a new executive and didn't have the five years of experience she had as an executive in public service. As she put it at an unusually testy press conference: "I know that he's a new executive of anything. So I can understand that anxiety…I can understand being anxious about wanting to get in there and to be of assistance."[4]

At the time, the media highlighted the mayor's swipe at Hogan's inexperience in defending her decision. The focus was on the political beef between them. But in looking back, I wonder: What if the National Guard had arrived sooner? Could they have helped to contain the protesters, demonstrators, and rioters and prevent the spread of violence? So, perhaps if things had been different—the Guard arriving sooner or the police not containing the students—maybe the eruption of Baltimore would not have happened at all. Certainly, right now there is no real way to tell.

Yet, had the Guard arrived sooner, maybe the rioting, burning, and looting wouldn't have happened or wouldn't have spread, regardless of what happened at Mondawmin. What if? What if? What if? I didn't know. But it is interesting to speculate.

In any case, Mayor Rawlings-Blake was under more fire over a controversial statement she had made. She said: "It's a very delicate balancing act because while we try to make sure that [the students] were protected from the cars and the other things that were going on, we also gave those who wished to destroy space to do that as well, and we work very hard to keep that balance and to put ourselves in the best position to de-escalate."[5]

One can only wonder: What was she thinking? Immediately the criticism about her statement spread on the social media.

One Twitter commentator observed: "Incompetent beyond belief…The mayor of Baltimore should be charged immediately for inciting a riot."

The mayor irritated the situation even more in her Monday night news conference when she tried to explain that she was asking the police to give the "peaceful demonstrators room to share their message," though unfortunately, that also gave those seeking to incite violence the space to operate. Worse, she used the word "thug" as she explained: "It is idiotic to think that by destroying your city, you're going to make life better for anybody…Too many people have spent generations building up this city for it to be destroyed by thugs who, in a very senseless way, are trying to tear down what so many have fought for."

In short, not only did the delay in calling the National Guard and the police confrontation at the mall contribute to more protesting, demonstrating, and unrest, but so did the remarks made by Mayor Rawlings-Blake.

In retrospect, it's hard to know what would have happened if any of these incidents had occurred differently or not at all. Perhaps some other spark might have ignited the uprising, since the well of anger was already there.

The Interview on What Was Happening in Baltimore

During this time, I was concerned about the kids in the city. I worried there would be a child or young teenager injured or worse during the unrest. To help make sense of what was happening, later that day a television news producer from the NBC News affiliate at WBAL-TV Baltimore called me to come into the studio for a live interview. What did I think about the uprising and the response from the city? I was sure the entire town would be watching. I felt I needed to speak from the heart and say something that could make a difference. Baltimore was in a real crisis and I was hoping that no one was either killed by the police or by the emotion-filled people in the streets. The situation was intense and the city needed to come together. Here is a transcript from that interview.

Debra Weiner: This is Kevin Shird, and he is a national youth advocate. Grew up in Baltimore. Nice to see you. You were telling me that when you were younger, you were one of these kids.

Kevin Shird: I was one of these kids. In and out of trouble, in the streets, making bad decisions.

Debra Weiner: You served about twelve years in federal prison?

Kevin: Almost twelve yes, yes. I started dealing drugs at age sixteen, so West Baltimore is my neighborhood. I know these kids very well who were engaged in this madness yesterday. They're not horrible kids, but they…did something pretty stupid…and they can be saved and I don't think that term "thug" is a great description.

Debra: To save the town, what's the next step?

Kevin: Be supportive. We need to continue to mentor the [kids]. We need to [help] them to get their education, because that's the key to success. Education and…we need to understand that a lot of these kids are dealing with pain. A lot of these kids have substance-abusing parents. A lot of these kids are dealing with their own personal issues, so you're talking about sixteen, seventeen, fifteen-year-old kids, and they're just dealing with the real issues of growth that a regular kid should have to deal with, and…you throw poverty on top of that, unemployment, parents struggling, substance abuse, they're dealing with some real issues…and I really hope that we can get back to that issue.

Debra: Well, I know you're concerned about that, because now we have…basically two very important conversations taking place. But I know you're concerned that the focus is away from the issue of police brutality.

Kevin: Yeah, so we need to talk about poverty [and] what was the effects of poverty…on these kid's behavior, coming from these tough neighborhoods, and [that goes] back to the Freddie Gray issue. These beat down, tore up neighborhoods…are struggling with unemployment, poverty, and that has a lot to do with how the police deal with the individuals in these neighborhoods. The police don't deal with an individual in Upper Park Heights the same

	way they would deal with an individual from Pennsylvania Avenue. It's a lot different. So you can't say poverty's not a factor in that whole scenario.
Debra:	As someone who works with young people, what would you say to someone right now who is looking at this and feeling a sense of hopelessness and perhaps not having great faith in how some of these investigations may pan out? What would you say?
Kevin:	I'd [say] be patient, give it time. I feel confident that these officers will be brought to justice. This is a national issue now. It's not just a Baltimore issue, so we've got the whole world watching. We got the White House watching, we got the Justice Department here in Baltimore [paying attention]. This is not an issue that they're going to be able to sweep under the rug, and… why would they? These [officers] are bad seeds. If these officers actually did this to this twenty-five-year-old man, they need to be brought to justice.
Debra:	Do you have faith in the political leaders in this city?
Kevin:	I know where their compassion lies. I met with the mayor and the police, and the commissioner last week before the incident happened over the weekend and yesterday. I know where

their hearts lie, and I know their passion is real. And hopefully that passion will be the driving force that helps them in their job.

Debra: We've been talking a lot about the power of the clergy in this situation. Do you feel in many ways that they can…help move this situation forward in a positive way?

Kevin: Yes, because they have a huge influence in the community. They're respected in the community, and their voice is a voice that many people listen to. So I think they'll be a factor.

Debra: In your own words, you said to me before we started that you were a young knucklehead… so I asked you, if you were out on the streets in the last day or so and if you were of that age… how do you think you would've responded?

Kevin: To be honest with you, at that age I was so… lost, I was misguided. I grew up with a substance-abusing parent myself, so there's a chance that I might have been one of those young kids. Running around, doing…negative things. My hope is that these kids have someone positive in their life. A teacher, a parent, a sister, a cousin, who can guide them through this storm, and hopefully this [protesting] won't be the thing that destroys the rest of their life, because yesterday hopefully was a hiccup and that won't continue.

Debra: Well, thank you for talking to us. Over to you guys in the back.

Stan Stovall: Yeah, very insightful, Mr. Shird. Thanks for joining us and offering insight. Especially from the perspective of you growing up here in those neighborhoods, where you know a lot of those kids and you know how they think and act.

Donna Hamilton: He knows what it's like to be one of those kids, and…he put it so well because when you're just a sixteen-[or]-seventeen-year-old kid, that's really difficult all by itself. Then you add in all those other negative things, that's a lot to deal with.

Stan Stovall: It's very easy as a spectator to say, "Why can't you just straighten up?" or "Why can't you just go to school?" and not be aware of some of the issues that Mr. Shird is speaking about that are going on in these kids' lives. It's easy not to be aware [of] the social economic issues that shatter their lives.

CHAPTER 3
1968

Though the violence in the city subsided, the scale of the marches and protests was reminiscent of the 1968 riots. The people had been energized in a way I had never seen in my life in Baltimore. Their emotion was raw and the protesters' passion to make a difference was unwavering. They were bent on being heard by the decision-makers of Baltimore. But, I wondered, would their actions finally be the glue to unify the city for forever? Or was the hard-won unity just another moment in time?

Although I didn't hear much about the 1968 riots in Baltimore before April 27, as the anger over Freddie Gray's death exploded, I thought about what had happened in Baltimore in 2015 and considered the parallels. The riots back then were never a hot topic of discussion in my world or among my peers, although history told a different story. Though I knew that in 1968 Martin Luther King, Jr., was assassinated, in my mind, I never connected the dots with Baltimore.

But now people were talking about that terrible day of April 4, 1968, and its parallels with the uprising in Baltimore. I learned from speaking with men and women in Baltimore who remembered those days well. While the MLK riots were sparked by the assassination of the iconic leader and Freddie Gray was a struggling youth in the inner city, they still saw the parallels in the roots of injustice, poverty, and hopelessness of the community.

As I realized from my conversations with the old heads in the community, it is important for everyday people—like myself and others—to think about the parallels between then and now.

It seemed prophetic that we had that conversation in April, since I had recently gone on a speaking engagement in Memphis, Tennessee. On March 6, just a few weeks before the uprising in Baltimore, I visited the infamous Lorraine Motel where Dr. King was assassinated, now a museum. Earlier in that day I spoke at the LeMoyne-Owens College and signed copies of my book, Lessons of Redemption, for students. While speaking at the college I described to students how as a teen I sold heroin on the streets of Baltimore and dropped out of high school to become a fulltime hustler. But I also discussed my road to redemption after spending several years in prison and how I used that time to transform myself by taking college courses. I explained that studying and reading in prison helped me grow and cope with my own demons of the past. That period of my life actually gave me the tools to reach young people struggling to find their own path in life. Hopefully a path for good.

My visit to the college in Memphis was incredible. I could remember my own past and path to transformation and experience the Lorraine Motel museum where history was made forty-seven years ago when the country was transformed. As I walked around the museum, the feeling of being in a place where a man was murdered, especially one as influential as Martin Luther King, Jr., was powerful. For me this visit became a history lesson about the year 1968 in America.

Seeing Memphis shortly before the Baltimore uprising and later thinking about the parallels was eerie for me. When I returned home to Baltimore, I didn't realize I would soon be receiving another history lesson in the making. The spirit of transformation was spreading throughout Baltimore. There was new hope for the future—much the way there had been in 1968, when the hope for what might be possible following a tragedy was in the air. After the murder of Dr. King, America was moved in ways she had never been before.

Comparing What Happened Then and Now

How was what the April 2015 uprising in Baltimore like what happened in April 1968? How was it different? And to what extent did what happened in 1968 provide the groundwork for what happened in 2015? I wanted to look more closely at this.

I discovered that Leon Neyfahk of *Slate* had written a comparison,[6] in which he found many parallels, and differences. As he wrote in his April 27 article, when the city caught fire, some people were already wondering whether the uprising would be "as devastating to the city as the long and deadly riot that engulfed it in the spring of 1968." Back then, the rioting—which led to six deaths and seven hundred injured,—was set off by the assassination of Martin Luther King, Jr., on Thursday, April 4. And much like the uprising of 2015, it began as a peaceful demonstration, but grew into something more dangerous on the night of Saturday, April 6, after a few fires were set and some windows were broken. However, in contrast to Mayor D'Alesandro, who immediately established an 11:00 p.m. curfew in 1968, Mayor Rawlings-Blake waited for some hours before calling in the National Guard and establishing a curfew.

Yet the 1968 uprising was much more damaging, because about a thousand small businesses were destroyed, compared to the few hundred cars and a dozen or so buildings burned in April 2015. Moreover, back in 1968, people burned down infrastructure and neighborhoods, and some businesses never returned, so scars from 1968 remained. Some areas hit hardest by the 2015 unrest have sections within them that haven't been rebuilt since the 1968 riots, according to an *NBC News* article: "Baltimore Riots: Violence Scarred a City Dealing with Decline for Decades," published April 29.[7]

But there are parallels in the way it took time for the anger to build into violent demonstrations and riots. For example, after Reverend King was assassinated on Thursday night, April 4, 1968, violence broke out that same night in many other cities in the United States. But initially Baltimore was calm. On Friday and most of Saturday in 1968, there were peaceful marches, while the fires and looting only started later on Saturday night. Then, on Sunday, the violence exploded and lasted for a week, though it is unclear what started the escalation. Likewise, for some time after Freddie Gray's death on April 19, 2015, the protests were relatively peaceful, though this period of protesting went on for about a week, versus the two days in 1968. But in both cases, the anger exploded and led to burning buildings and looting, plus over a hundred burning cars in Baltimore in 2015.

Neyfahk also spoke to Elizabeth M. Nix, an assistant professor at the University of Baltimore and a co-editor of the 2011 book, *Baltimore '68: Riots and Rebirth in an American City*, to get insights on the parallels between the root causes of the riots, then and now. In her view, many of the triggers were the same, coming from Baltimore's long history of racial segregation and poverty. As she told Neyfahk:

There are parallels in that the makings of the '68 riots came long in advance of the uprisings themselves. A lot of the industrial profits the city had enjoyed during World War II had started to dry up, and a lot of people started to move to the suburbs. So, a lot of people were seeing their city get poorer. Baltimore had also been suffering for many decades from racial segregation... so there were residential covenants that kept black people out of certain neighborhoods.

That had been going on for decades in Baltimore, and in '68, many of the neighborhoods affected by it just exploded. And some of those are the same neighborhoods that are suffering the effects of today's violence."[8]

A look at the statistics from the 1960s and '70s and today shows how the conditions of poverty and racial injustice that contributed to the riots then, continued and even worsened, though the destruction today wasn't as bad as then. These patterns are starkly described in a *Think Progress* article by Bryce

Covert, "The Economic Devastation Fueling the Anger in Baltimore."[9] As Covert writes, Freddie Gray grew up in a neighborhood that was especially plagued by the problems that have long faced Baltimore. In his Sandtown-Winchester neighborhood, more than half the people between sixteen and sixty-four are out of work and the one-in-five unemployment rate is double that of the city as a whole. With a median income of $24,000, well below the poverty line for a family of four, nearly a third of the families in this neighborhood live in poverty, while a quarter to a third of the buildings are vacant, compared to five percent in the city as a whole.

Covert points out how all of these conditions—high unemployment, low incomes, and widespread foreclosure—have a long history in Baltimore, dating back to the 1960s and '70s. A key reason is the collapse of the steel industry, which was a large contributor to the thriving economy in Baltimore when Bethlehem Steel opened at Sparrow Point in the early 1900s. The industry boomed during World War II. It had 35,000 workers at its peak in 1959. But by 1968, when Reverend King was assassinated, the industry and economy of Baltimore was already in decline. Then, in the early '70s, the Sparrows Point plant laid off three thousand workers in 1971 and another seven thousand in 1975. By the '80s, only eight thousand of those 35,000 jobs still existed, and in all the city lost over a hundred thousand manufacturing jobs between 1950 and 1995.

All of this manufacturing decline contributed to the conditions in Baltimore today, since, as Covert notes, "the city never really recovered from that loss and the effects can still be seen today." Moreover, the march of history has been especially devastating for Baltimore's black population. For example, the share of employed black men between sixteen to sixty-four dropped more than 15 percent, from about three-quarters employed in 1970 to just 57.5 percent by 2010, whereas more than three-quarters of white men were employed. As Covert points out: "That racial gap has grown steadily since the 1970s, from a 10 percentage point difference in how many men had work, to a 20 percentage point one."

Making matters worse, this economic decline over the past fifty years has been paired with "white flight," as occurred in other cities that have experienced unrest, like Ferguson, Missouri. While Baltimore's black population nearly doubled between 1950 and 1970, the whites moved away. Almost one third of the city's population fled the city between 1950 and 2000, according to Covert.

Moreover, real estate agents helped further the "white flight" by playing up racial fears and worries about falling property values. Those fears, in turn, led white residents who lived near expanding black neighborhoods to sell their houses. But as all homeowners do, they tried to get as much for their homes as possible, since houses are an investment. But it's ironic when you think about it. At a time when the neighborhood was becoming home to poorer and poorer families, those who lived there were paying more.

At the same time, predatory lenders were developing relationships with churches and community groups, so they persuaded homeowners with good credit to take out loans with higher interest rates than they should have paid. At the same time, they enticed people with low incomes who couldn't afford loans to take out mortgages without any down payments or any paperwork showing their income. So no wonder the foreclosure rates shot sky high, forcing people out of their homes. And no wonder the anger was building in the community.

Thus, while the trigger point for the riots in 1968 and 2015 might have been different—the assassination of a much-loved leader of the people in 1968—the death of a low-income unemployed young man from injuries sustained a police van in 2015—the underlying conditions of poverty, racial discrimination, and injustice were the same. Certainly, in 2015, conditions were better, but the baseline of poverty and racial barriers was the same. Consider the 2015 and 1968 comparison to be a kind of "same old, same old" story.

In my research, I found even more numbers that tell the story, like an *Al Jazeera America* report on "Baltimore: The Divided City Where Freddie Gray Lived and Died."[10] According to the article, "Baltimore has long experienced high poverty rates. But those figures soar when filtered through the prisms of locality and race," in that inequality increases in the predominantly black neighborhoods of West Baltimore, where this week's unrest was primarily seen. As this article points out, because of historic housing discrimination, the foreclosure crisis, and white flight from poor neighborhoods in Baltimore's predominantly black inner city, the number of abandoned houses grew from seven thousand in 1970 to forty thousand in 1998. Now, vacant homes make up 13 percent of the total housing stock.

These changes in Baltimore led to the city's public schools becoming "hyper-segregated by race," so that since the 1960s, the school population has been overwhelmingly black and poor. Though black individuals make up 64 percent of the city, we make up 85 percent of K-12 classrooms, and the majority of public school students qualify for free or reduced meals because they come from impoverished families. And, commonly, young people attend schools with underfunded and decaying facilities.

Still another problem is that the decline of jobs in Baltimore has led to a declining tax base to pay for city services, including education and police training. That then sets in motion a vicious cycle, because when services deteriorate, it becomes more difficult to attract business investment, and those left behind have to pay even more taxes. As urban policy experts and economists point out, it becomes very difficult to stop this vicious cycle of decline, because "shrinking job opportunities further widen income disparities and inequality."[11]

This dire picture has only gotten worse since '68, creating an even deeper pool of anger and stress. Though the 2015 uprising didn't result in as much damage as those in 1968—perhaps because of the presence of the National Guard and the 10:00 p.m. curfew—the conditions that gave rise to this anger have continued. So, another spark might ignite these fires again one day and cause even more damage, unless something is done to fix the problems we face.

So now more than ever, this comparison of Baltimore in 1968 and 2015 shows the need to recognize what it costs to have a divided Baltimore and why we must even out the income disparities. It is not enough to simply point out that conditions have deteriorated since the '70s. The new cycle of riots in the same neighborhoods affected by the riots nearly fifty years ago—and in neighborhoods where scars from the '68 riots still remain in the form of burned down homes and stores not rebuilt—shows the urgent need to act now. It is even more urgent in Baltimore, as in other cities characterized by disparities of wealth and poverty, to change before the anger boils over again. All it takes is another trigger incident to release the anger and pain like an erupting volcano, destroying everything in its path.

CHAPTER 4
ANOTHER PERSPECTIVE

On April 29, I was contacted by the CNN network to be interviewed on my perspective of the Baltimore uprising and riots. This is when I really began to understand the full magnitude of the unrest and violence here in the city. The world was hungry for answers and wanted to know: Why Baltimore? And why now? Here are the highlights of that conversation with CNN anchor Carol Costello.

Carol Costello: My next guest knows the city well and the challenges many here face. Kevin Shird grew up in West Baltimore. He's a former drug dealer who traded the tough streets for a brand new life. In addition to being a community leader focused on substance abuse prevention, he is the author of *Lessons of Redemption*. Kevin, thanks so much for being here. Can we talk about the "thug" word? Because I was out last night with a young lady and she gave me a tongue lashing for about forty minutes…She said that I should not have called the people who burned down the CVS store "idiots." Help me understand that.

Kevin Shird: I can see how that could be offensive. They are definitely criminal acts, no doubt about that. I'm not here to make excuses for that. But when you have people that's been living in poverty for a long time and unemployment—you have a 50 percent unemployment rate in that area. We're talking about people stuck on substance abuse, some with mental health issues… They're not idiots. They're human beings, but they also need help.

Carol Costello: Well, when you have the Crips coming out and saying that people shouldn't have looted the CVS store, that says something, right? I also understand what this young woman was trying to say to me. She said, "…we're powerless. We don't have money…We live in a poverty-stricken area."

Kevin: Right.

Carol: Probably don't have the best education, we have no power, so how else do we seize that power, right?

Kevin: We need to continue to focus in on education, poverty, and unemployment. Washington talks about these things all the time. For some reason, that message hasn't reached Pennsylvania Avenue and North Avenue, right? With an unemployment rate at 50 percent, anywhere else in America, those numbers would be absurd. The sad part about it is, we have protesters here that were actually focused on a real important issue, like police brutality, so it… overshadowed the more important issues.

Carol: That's exactly right. You heard what that one lawmaker said. He said that the "thug" word is just like the N-word. Is it?

Kevin: It's not like the N-word in my mind. It's been radicalized across America, so I could see why some people could become offended by that.

Carol: Well, even Jamal Bryant said that…it's like calling an African-American person the N-word, if you call an African-American person a thug. But, other people would say, if you're committing violent behavior, it doesn't matter what color you are, you're a thug.

Kevin: These were young juveniles, so in my mind, I don't see a sixteen-seventeen-year-old as a thug. I've seen thugs, and they don't look like thugs to me. However, we just want to stay focused on the issue of police brutality and the Freddie Gray matter, because this [has] distracted us from the political stuff that was really going on

	in this city. That [should] be the focus.
Carol:	Thanks so much for stopping by and…thank you so much for your book.

I walked away from the CNN set in front of city hall and spotted a couple National Guard troops at the corner of Holiday Street. It was all so surreal. These guys had probably been in Afghanistan and Iraq. Now they were standing guard on American soil, outside of city hall in downtown Baltimore. The city had been turned on its head and everyone was trying to figure out what happened and how we got here.

To understand why Baltimore suddenly blew up, look at how Baltimore has changed over the years, from when it was an industrial city in the shadow of Washington, DC, to when it became a city filled with racial tensions that blew up in the Freddie Gray case. To find out how Baltimore has changed, I spoke with David Nevins, a Baltimore resident of over forty years, who now lives in the suburbs. He has been a communications expert for more than thirty years. I've highlighted the major themes we talked about during our conversation, a very insightful conversation on his perspective. One thing I've learned about fixing problems is that you don't have to agree on how to fix the problem but you should at least understand the other person's viewpoint.

Growing Up in the Baltimore Area

David, what was it like growing up in Baltimore back in those days?

I was born in New York and raised in Montgomery County in Rockville, outside of Baltimore. I was the classic case of the underachiever in high school. When I graduated, a lot of my friends were going off to fancy colleges and universities, and I had great SAT scores, but my parents were not sure if I was going to be serious about college. My father was especially concerned. Even though we lived in Montgomery County, he had just taken a job with the government in health planning in downtown Baltimore, which is now known as State Center. He drove back and forth to Baltimore every day. Since he wanted to make sure I went to college, he told me there is this nice little college he heard of in a suburb of Baltimore called Towson, and I should check it out. I did. We visited it together and I thought it was a nice, friendly little place. So, in the fall of 1972, I moved into the dorms there.

Before then, since I grew up in Montgomery County, I had only been to Baltimore city two or three times. What I knew about it was the famous landmarks. It was home of Johns Hopkins University and Haussner's Restaurant, known back then for its German cooking.

When I went to college, about forty years ago, Baltimore was a lot different from today. Back then, it was a sleepy mid-Atlantic city. There was no Inner Harbor at the time. To get exercise, while I was at the university, my buddies and I, who were sports fans, would walk to the Memorial Stadium on Thirty-Third Street to see a baseball game. It took us about an hour to get to a game and an hour walk back. At the time, we felt entirely safe along the way, since the city was like a large small town with very little crime. So, I felt I could walk anywhere.

I stayed at Towson University for four years—the only member of my family to go to university in Baltimore. Though my father died early, my mother, brother, and sister still live in Montgomery County. After I moved to Towson to go to college, I never left the Baltimore area.

Early Days in Baltimore

David, what was it like in Baltimore four decades ago?

In the early 1970s, when I went to college at Towson, Baltimore was a racially diverse city. Despite the city's age, going back to revolutionary times, I viewed it as a young city that wasn't ready to come into its own yet, and some still claim it just exists in the shadows of its sister city to the south, Washington, DC, which is only forty-five minutes away.

Back then, it was a great place to go to college. We would walk to the bars, restaurants, shops, and movie theaters of Towson, and we would hop the bus on York Road to head into the city for a downtown visit. We referred to our university as the Harvard of York Road.

At the time, Baltimore was a blue-collar manufacturing city. While I was in my teens and early twenties, the Bethlehem Steel Corporation was alive and well and thriving, as was the Port of

Baltimore, with imports and exports that moved in and out on a daily basis. Johns Hopkins, both the university and hospital, were growing. There was a lot of small and light manufacturing. I even stayed in Baltimore in the summers, and I lived in an upstairs little apartment on Harford Road at Northern Parkway.

I took the number 55 bus to my summer internship at Towson in 1972, four years after the 1968 riots. Along the way, I passed all kinds of businesses that, in the forty years since, appear to have gone away. I didn't see any remnants of the riots in the form of broken windows and burnt-down buildings. But it wasn't yet a vibrant city, since there were not a great number of downtown area restaurants, not that I could have afforded them as a student. As I recall, the Mechanic Theater was being built or about to be built. It was still a working-class city.

What impressed me is that people loved their city, because when I would tell people that I graduated college and was staying in Baltimore, my cousins in Denver, Colorado, and Miami would say, "What? Why?" because their cities at the time were viewed as much more vibrant and exciting. Baltimore had not yet hit its stride.

Race Relationships

David, what were race relationships like at that time in Baltimore, in this post-civil rights era?

At the time, I was only twenty-one or twenty-two years old, so it is not one of the things that I followed, since Towson University was my world. It was 90 percent Caucasian, and maybe even a little bit more. I was the president of the student body and we funded the establishment. There was a group of young black students—at a time when the "African-American" term hadn't yet been invented—who wanted to promote and preserve black culture on campus. They founded our campus first black student union. Though we were all friendly with one another, we had an occasional budgetary battle and they wanted more money. As the president of student body, I had a lot of control over a little bit of money.

So ironically, the students there were in a stronger position than they were in the rest of Baltimore. That's my sad impression of the situation. For Baltimore has never struck me, then or now, as a place where whites and blacks mingle routinely. That is, now as then, you have your white places, you have your black places. You occasionally go to an event or to a restaurant that's 90 percent white and 10 percent black, maybe on occasion 80 percent white, 20 percent black, but very rarely, in my experience, is it 50 percent white, 50 percent black in Baltimore. So, the Baltimore of forty years ago still looks much the same as Baltimore today. I'm really not sure why this is.

Why is that, David? Was it race, class, wealth? How do these factors contribute?

I think the answer to this sixty-four-million-dollar question is a failure of society. It's bigger than you and me. Individually, we may all be good or want to be, and other than the difference in our skin colors, we're pretty much all the same. Obviously, there are significant vestiges of racism. But these differences are not really about black versus white or black and white. It's really about cultural and economic differences, which apply then and today.

For example, the wealthy blacks that I know in Baltimore associate routinely and are welcomed with open arms in the white community from my experiences.

Ironically, I'm the president of the Center Club, which is Baltimore's premier downtown dining and business club, founded fifty-four years ago, around 1960. It was founded because the visionary business leaders at that time found there were no clubs where they could all come together. There was not a single club, although there were a dozen different business clubs in town at the time. So, these guys got together and founded the Center Club. There were clubs that didn't admit blacks, others that didn't admit Jews, and clubs that didn't admit women. So, they founded the Center Club in about 1960 to break the barrier and bring people together.

I'm incredibly honored and fortunate today to be the president of the Center Club today. Ninety percent of those other clubs are falling by the wayside, since there is no room today in Baltimore for clubs that discriminate, while the Center Club is thriving. It's made up of the upper stratosphere, though these people shouldn't really be called the privileged, because most of these people have worked hard to get to the top. For example, I consider myself a significant business and civic leader, but I wasn't privileged, since I worked very hard to get where I am. Now it seems there is much more coming together and intermingling of people who are at the top, like business owners, CEOs, lawyers, doctors, and other influential people.

Socializing across racial groups seems a lot more fluid. White kids probably have more African-American friends than their parents had. And now when you go to the malls, seeing mixed couples is a regular occurrence.

So, what that means to me is that if kids are under thirty, they are pretty close to color-blind in terms of who their friends are, who they date, and who they socialize and hang out with. Whereas for those older than thirty, that seems not at all to be the case. You can see that all over, in places like Towson University, in the malls, in the Inner Harbor. So, I guess we are making a little bit of progress.

The Bright Lights of Baltimore Before the Unrest

From your perspective, David, before pockets of the city erupted in violence in April 2015, what was Baltimore like in your view?

It seemed like Baltimore was finally becoming a shining, bright light. I thought to myself that for the first time in a long time, Baltimore was really on the move. The city was on fire in that it was getting recognized all around the globe as the place young millennials were choosing to grow up in. Though I was surprised, given Baltimore's sleepy history, I was incredibly impressed by this transformation.

We even had a young woman working at the firm who published an op-ed in one of the national newspapers describing how her post-college friends were choosing to move to Baltimore as the place to be. They moved primarily downtown and to Federal Hill,

Fells Point, Canton, Patterson Park, and Mount Vernon. They came to Baltimore in droves to work in the tech industry, our booming healthcare industry, and other high-growth industries. And a great many new restaurants opened, every day it seemed a new restaurant was opening. Yet the demand from the newcomers was so great that these restaurants were even all full at the same time.

Thus, through early 2014 to early 2015, it seems like it was really Baltimore's time. The spotlight was shining on our city for the first time in a long, long time. That's the shame of what was about to happen.

What was the attitude or feeling in the business community at the time, from your perspective, David? What were business leaders talking about regarding expanding their businesses, going into new businesses, or employing more people?

While the mood was upbeat in the pre–Freddie Gray era, looking back post–Freddie Gray, there were still a lot of things missing in the city. I think we were thrilled to see the city get the kind of recognition that it deserved. Yet the city was still recovering from the recession of a few years earlier, so many of my business associates called it a "fragile" city. It was fragile because the new businesses were mostly smaller ones. Yes, restaurants, stores, and shops were opening, apartment complexes were being built at a record pace for Baltimore, and condos were being sold. Yet, large businesses still were not moving here.

Do you mean the big box stores, like the Walmart and Fortune 500 companies?

Yes. Though stores were opening, corporate headquarters weren't. For example, Walmart was building stores here, but the company wasn't manufacturing here what was sold in the stores. As for the corporate headquarters of the Fortune 500 companies, we don't have any of those in Baltimore and haven't had them for over a decade.

Another reason this is a fragile economy is because the people moving here or already here are largely working in service jobs, since Baltimore has been shifting from a manufacturing economy to a service economy in the last twenty years. But a service economy is a much more fragile economy than a manufacturing economy. That's a problem, because people in those jobs get paid less than if they worked in manufacturing. So, they don't have as much to spend, like in the new restaurants in Baltimore. People have to make enough money somewhere to frequent those places. But if they aren't making enough, they won't go there, so those businesses could readily open and quickly die.

For example, at one time, many members of my family worked at Bethlehem Steel when Baltimore used to be a steel city. But Bethlehem Steel employs zero people in Baltimore today. Ironically, at a time when Baltimore was a big steel-manufacturing city, a big rivalry developed in football between the Baltimore and the Pittsburgh Steelers because Baltimore and Pittsburgh were viewed as the same type of city for the last hundred years. Today, Pittsburgh still has some steel and other manufacturing, but Baltimore has virtually none. The football rivalry remains alive and well, which is a good thing. But the two cities have gone their separate ways.

Who would you say are the biggest employers in Baltimore?

The biggest employers in Baltimore are now educational and healthcare institutions. Johns Hopkins University and hospital is far and away number one; the University of Maryland is number two. Another healthcare chain, MedStar Health, is number three. If you go through the list of top-ten employers, which are very prominent successful organizations, they employ about two hundred thousand people, and not one of these companies manufactures anything. The companies do good things, since they make people healthy and educate people, but these are all services. And service industry jobs pay lower wages and they can readily disappear when conditions change.

Lost Business Opportunities in the Post–Freddie Gray Era

What kind of scars and lost business opportunities does Baltimore face in the post–Freddie Gray era, David?

After the uprising and the controversy about how the situation was handled, Baltimore suffered some scars, like lost business opportunities and conventions. A couple of conventions that had planned to come to Baltimore didn't, and there was a significant loss of business. The lost business would have been just a blip on the radar screen, in that cities around the country lose business for different reasons…Boston lost business because it had several feet of snow this past winter. And every city from time to time has a week when the restaurants are shut down completely or early because of some challenging natural event.

How were you affected personally during this shutdown?

In the short term, we lost a lot of business at the Center Club, since we closed for that week because our employees, who mostly live in the city and take public transportation to work, had to be home by 10:00 p.m. To make sure they got home in time, we had to shut down at 8:00 p.m., and since the average person or business group comes in for dinner at 7:00 p.m., we didn't have enough time to serve them before the employees would have to leave. So, we shut down for that week. We lost tens of thousands of dollars as a result, but we're a multimillion dollar operation, so we could absorb the loss.

But the individual restaurants and shops were much more severely affected. Each restaurant probably lost thousands, and the bigger ones probably lost tens of thousands of dollars. The shops similarly lost thousands of dollars each, while the bigger stores lost much more. But even those losses would be nothing but a blip on the radar screen, since the business can recover from that, and many businesses might get reimbursed by their insurance.

So what kinds of losses were more serious and long-lasting?

The biggest loss is the more long-term, lingering loss of business and reputation. Before the Freddie Gray riots, Baltimore was a city on the move. We were a city on fire. Now, the national perception of the city literally changed to a negative one. There is some irony in this changed perception about Baltimore, when you compare it to the way Boston bounced back after the bombing at the Boston Marathon. For several days, while the culprits were on the loose, businesses shut down. Then, this past winter, Boston had a major snowfall, so businesses were shut down too. However, as of today, Boston's reputation is as good, strong, and busy as ever. No one says, "I'm not going to go to Boston because of the bombing at the Boston Marathon." No one says, "I'm not going to go to Boston because of all the snow they got." In fact, the marathon actually got bigger the year after these two incidents. Perhaps Boston experienced this increase in interest because the two incidents helped people in the community rally together. They felt an outside event or natural disaster brought them together to protect their community.

But Baltimore suffered a reputational crisis, and that is much, much harder to fix, which I know since I'm in the marketing business. This crisis occurred because the Freddie Gray unrest wasn't regarded as a single incident that happened and is over. Rather, it is viewed as a situation that occurred because of a number of underlying causes which haven't yet been addressed. So, the damage goes much deeper because this view that Baltimore has a serious problem affects the people around the country who might want to visit here and might want to bring conventions here. It even affects the view of the suburban middle class and upper middle class community that for a long time has enjoyed going to the Inner Harbor, dining in Fells Point, dining in Canton, shopping, and enjoying other like experiences in Baltimore. But now they're all saying, "How do we know that another riot won't happen again tonight?" So, they're scared to do things because their attitude toward Baltimore has changed from an up-and-coming city to a place of potential danger.

The positive attitude toward Boston didn't change because the events that happened there were unexpected, unlikely, [one-time] events. But there are certain things that are unpredictable, that could happen again, which is what Baltimore is now suffering from. So, it won't be able to repair its business reputation until we have figured out the unpredictable, like when and if there will be another riot. So, how can we fix that? How can we assure people that we are a safe city?

What about having a national campaign to support the city, like the Boston Strong campaign that went across the country after the Boston Marathon, though that was in response to a terrorist attack? What do you think of that approach, David?

After the Freddie Gray uprising in Baltimore, Baltimore did start a campaign entitled One Baltimore. And that kind of campaign is the key to how we can move past this situation. First, of all, what happened in Baltimore could have happened in many major American cities, and this is one of those situations where we in Baltimore were unlucky. For example, a few months before the Freddie Gray incident, at Ferguson...that city was the unlucky one after the killing of Michael Brown by a white police officer triggered a series of riots. And those situations have been echoed in other cities, like the choking of Eric Garner in Staten Island. One incident in a city evokes a protest in response to similar underlying conditions, like the perception of racism.

But now the One Baltimore campaign could help to change perceptions in Baltimore, though it's in its infancy at this moment. I believe every cloud has a silver lining, and the silver lining here has not yet developed. But the opportunity to have a gigantic silver lining has developed through responding to the incident with a campaign to bring a new recognition to Baltimore as a thriving and safe city again.

Attitudes about Demonstrating and Rioting

What was the attitude of your employees at the Center Club during the incident? How did they feel about the Freddie Gray incident?

That's a good question, since our staff of about fifty people is about 50 percent black and 50 percent white, we would hear what the employees thought about the rioting, the looting, the burning of cars, and other things that happened during the riots from both sides.

For example, I remember one story from one of our young African-American employees. A key to his attitude about what happened is that he had a job, but my impression is that most of the people looting, rioting, and demonstrating didn't have jobs, and I would have been shocked to see any of our employees on a video looting a store, though they did grow up and many of them still live in those communities where many people are out of work. Well, one day I was having lunch with this employee, and I asked him, "What do you think of what's going on with these continued protests?" He said, "It's terrible. These protests and riots are bad for the city. They're bad for the community." Then he expressed the central point of this dilemma facing Baltimore when he said, "I'm glad I have this job, but I wish right now I could be there with them." He was talking about being with the demonstrators, because he, with a job, felt he was one of the lucky ones. He still felt like he should be supporting his brothers and sisters, who were the demonstrators, though he wasn't interested in supporting the looters.

From your perspective, David, how do people feel about the protests and demonstrations? It seems like a lot of the people protesting the issue had legitimate gripes and in America, you're free to protest, and one way to be heard is to put on demonstrations, which is lawful. How did the employees feel about this?

Certainly, there is a long tradition of peacefully protesting to get heard. I demonstrated myself when I was in my teens in Washington, DC, against the Vietnam War, with a million other people. I was the same age as the young man who said to me, "I wish I could be there with them." I was with them when they were demonstrating against a different social problem.

Though our employees weren't involved in the demonstrations, they did have feelings about what was going on in their communities, because this is where they and their families lived. So, they were impacted in many ways. Though most of our employees have been with us for a long time and are the best of the best, no matter where they live, they work in this beautiful, multimillion dollar renovated facility on the fifteenth floor overlooking a gorgeous city and Inner Harbor. So, they literally spend their daily lives in two different worlds. They interact every day not only with their work colleagues, but with the business and civic leaders of the community.

Just working at the Center Club makes their lives different than the lives of their colleagues at home, who might be, if lucky, working in the local shoe store or service job, because there are so few manufacturing jobs in the city. Thus, our employees were often torn because of what happened and felt awful about the situation. It was a strange time.

It's a complicated subject because the demonstrations brought out many differences in attitudes and issues that hadn't been expressed before. It brought up a divide between groups, like when we had to wonder what people from different groups were thinking.

The Uniqueness of the Situation Today

It seems like one thing that made these protests difficult for people is that most people in Baltimore haven't experienced anything like this before in their lives. So this was something new and people didn't know how to assess the situation. What do you think, David?

That's true. It was a totally new situation. People watched it on television throughout the world—in England, in Brazil, in South Korea, everywhere. But there's no playbook for a citizen on what to do when it comes to the issue of an uprising, disturbance, demonstration, looting, or burning cars in your community.

Certainly, the country had a number of incidents, like the 1968 riots in San Francisco and later the Rodney King protests in Los Angeles in 1991. More recently, we had the protests and riots in Ferguson, Missouri, and in some cities, like Oakland, where sympathizers organized protests. But we haven't had what has happened in Baltimore for forty-seven years. So, for the most part, you have to be over sixty years old to remember anything similar to that here.

So, about 80 percent of America never experienced this kind of mass uproar. In recent years, we have experienced watching riots and demonstrations in Egypt and in countries that have dictators or are at war. But we haven't experienced that kind of turmoil in our own backyard in recent years. So, I think it was really mind blowing and surreal that this situation developed at home. But if we don't forget about it and move on too quickly… what happened can serve as a blueprint to fix Baltimore and to fix America.

A Historical Perspective

How about putting this in a historical perspective, David?

Certainly. I'm a little bit of a history buff and if you follow history, most governments don't survive for more than a couple or a few hundred years before there's a revolution. We're a couple of hundred years old now, since the revolution that founded our nation and we had the Civil War over the issue of slavery.

Unfortunately, we haven't as much as we would've hoped since then, so it's hard to tell if the racial protests sweeping the nation today represent the very small beginnings of a revolution. The sad part is that today's struggle is over essentially the same thing as happened back in 1968. It's over people who feel they have been treated by our government as second class citizens. It's not necessarily whites versus blacks, but class versus class.

Blacks and Hispanics are typically targeted for exploitation and injustice. So, inequality—the huge gap between the wealth and the underserved—is at the heart of the struggles and the protests sweeping the nation today.

With that said, what did you think when you saw the uprising in Ferguson last year? And in another similar situation, an unarmed black man died in the custody of the police in Staten Island. Later in 2014, there were massive marches and demonstrations in New York City over Eric Garner's choking death.

For some, it was eerily similar to the civil rights era in the disconnect between the police and the community that has contributed to antipathy on both sides, though we may not know all the facts in these particular cases. For example, since these incidents didn't occur in Baltimore, I felt that I really didn't completely know what happened in New York or Ferguson. In New York, an overzealous officer put a black man into a chokehold and killed him. I don't think the officer intended to kill him, but he killed him. He was wrong and what he did was inappropriate, since he apparently exhibited undue force. Likewise, the incident in Ferguson raises many more questions about police misconduct.

It's clear, in this country we have a problem with the training and the attitude of some police officers, but you can't put the blame for the problem solely on the police, because you also have an antagonistic relationship between the community and the police. It's a little bit like the classic chicken and egg question. Just like I don't know which came first, the chicken or the egg, I don't know which came first in the police-community conflict. Whichever came first, the problem exists today and we need to work hard to fix it.

The Problem of Profiling

Do you think profiling contributes to the problem, David?

That's an interesting question, because there are different views about this. The liberals among us say, "Profiling? That's a terrible thing," right? Well, you know what? It is a terrible thing when it is used to unjustifiably subject someone to mistreatment at the hands of law enforcement. But I don't know anyone who does not want profiling to take place when you get on an airplane, like when they pull you out of the line to make sure you aren't a terrorist. For example, when they pull me, my wife, or my friend who are all white, out of the line, and they take us aside and pat us down for an extra five minutes, we all say: "Why are you taking me out of the line?" We think that someone else is the person you should be looking at. I'm not saying that person is actually a terrorist, but we think the guy has that look, because he has a beard or the woman…because she's wrapped up. In other words, we ask why the agents have chosen us to check out rather than someone else who we think fits the terrorist profile.

We have this split attitude, because we live in a world where on the one hand you want profiling to keep you safe. On the other hand, you don't want profiling because it's unfair. And blacks are often targeted by profiling which is very unfair. How do we fix this?

The Unexpected Eruption in Baltimore

The underlying signs of growing problems were there, like in the growing class inequality and the problems with profiling. But when it comes to the actual eruption of protests and rioting, I don't think anybody saw this coming for Baltimore. I think over the years we felt the tension, but I don't think anybody in Ferguson said, "Well, Baltimore's next." What do you think, David?

I agree, we didn't expect that to happen. I think we felt the pain that many people were experiencing in these other cities… But I agree with you that we had no idea that our community would be next. It does feel a little like 1968 again, since the 1960s were a time when we had the assassinations of Robert Kennedy, Martin Luther King, Malcolm X, and John F. Kennedy. I didn't relate to what was happening at the time because I was just a kid. I didn't have the social consciousness or awareness that I have today. But I think what happened in Baltimore has made us more socially conscious and aware today.

Yet, ironically, what happened was a freaky thing. If not for the wrong sharp turn that the policeman took or but for speeding, Freddie Gray might not have been killed. What happened was a freaky thing because in every urban area in America, from time to time, the police stop someone for a minor infraction. But this time it resulted in the killing of Freddie Gray in Baltimore where we live.

KEVIN SHIRD

CHAPTER 5
POVERTY AND PAIN

After another long day, I headed home for the night, thinking about how the poverty and pain I see all around the city contrasted with what my life had now become. Though I had grown up in the jungle of the Baltimore streets, from the time I pledged to do things differently, the opportunities have been tremendous. I had this urge to do something better with my life and I wasn't satisfied with being just another statistic.

Like many others in the working class I had to cope with long work hours and no days off, but I was thankful for my new success and wouldn't trade it for the world. But now I clearly see the stark contrast between the life I have now and the life where so many people in the inner city felt trapped. Many still believe that there is no way out, no way to erase the pain. When a man can't see a future for himself it dehumanizes him. It weighs him down and impedes his growth.

As I reflected on these thoughts, my cell phone rang and an unfamiliar telephone number appeared. Since it was pass 10:30 p.m., I almost didn't answer the call, feeling that it was time to shut things down for the night. Although my life had changed in many ways, I was still struggling to find that balance between work and leisure time. But I answered, and on the line was a voice from my days on the streets—and he probably wouldn't have called back. The highlights of our conversation went like this:

"Hello."

Then the unidentified caller said, "Hello, can I speak with Kevin?"

After I identified myself the caller said, "This is Twin from Mount Street. You told me to call you when I'm ready, man."

"You right, bro, I did say that…"

"Seriously, I can't do this no more, Kev. I'm ready to do something different, man. I can't do this street shit no more, bro. It's crazy out here, man. Motherfuckers robbing and killing each other every day over nothing. I'm ready to get out! I want to do the shit you doing, man. I want to help kids and shit like that. I want to talk to kids about staying out of these fucking streets and out of the game. This ain't no way to live man."

Yet, as much as Twin might want to leave the streets, I knew he had to be completely ready to move on. He had to truly reform himself first. There's a difference between wanting something and taking the steps to make it happen. There's a difference between having a dream and actualizing it. So, I tried to explain to Twin what he needed to do.

"It's great to want to help kids, bro, but first you gotta help yourself. You gotta make sure you're good first before you can help anybody else turn things around."

"I'm good right now, bro. I'm ready now."

"Look man, I'll definitely look out for you, but you have to be willing to listen and learn. At some point you can definitely work with kids. You have a lot to offer. But you have to get all the way out of those streets first, bro. You have to get out the game and stay out. A lot of guys get out the streets but they're still holding onto the street mentality. You have to let go of all that shit. That street code bullshit doesn't apply in the real world. You can't be telling kids they have to change but you also telling them to live by the street's code. They know a contradiction when they hear one."

"I get it, man. I get it. And it's time, Kev. I can't do this shit no more, man."

But while Twin might have thought he was ready, he had a lot of work to do first. "Look, give me a call in the morning bro. I need you to call my man, Moses Hammett. He's been working in workforce development for years helping ex-offenders get their shit in order. He's good people. The first thing we need to do is get you a job somewhere. Even when you trying to change your life you still have to eat."

"I just don't want to no bullshit job making pennies, man. I still want to have my dignity."

"Brother, right now you need to be willing to do whatever you can. Right now I'm just trying to save your life. Moses can definitely help you get on your feet. He helped me almost ten years ago and I haven't looked back since."

We hung up and I had the sense that Twin was unlikely to take that next step. It's like he wanted it all now, but wasn't ready to put in the self-work to really turn things around. He still struck me as the street hustler I had known from my own days in the game. Now he just wanted a different kind of hustle, where he come feel like a human being again. I planned to do everything I could to get him on the right track. I sensed that he wouldn't do everything I asked of him, but I hoped I was wrong.

• • • • • •

The concrete jungle, also known as urban America, is a harsh place to live for many people. When one looks at some of the poorest streets of Baltimore, it's hard to believe that people actually live here. The depression, the blight, and the despair is everywhere, and overwhelming to all who live there. This is ground zero where the everyday struggle to survive in the middle of poverty and violence can have a debilitating hold on human life. This is the ugly side of America, where many live, but most would rather stay far away from.

As I drove around the city in the days after the Freddie Gray protests and riots, I had felt this despair, especially when I was in the streets of the Sandtown-Winchester, where Gray had lived. I saw the vacant faces of my people sitting on stoops, the joyless eyes of teenagers hanging out by the corner stores, the grim stares of children playing in front of their homes. On seeing their faces, I felt the pain of poverty, I felt the pain of lost hopes and dreams, and I felt the fear they lived with every day. They faced the month-to-month threat of eviction, should an illness or injury deprive them of the small amount of money earned from a low-wage job. And, even scarier, they faced the everyday danger of being shot by an errant bullet from a gun battle on the street.

I decided to explore the painful truths of poverty to better understand its side effects. I began with some of the key indicators: the 50 percent poverty and 50 percent unemployment rate in Sandtown-Winchester and the effects of poverty on the adults and on the development of children. I also looked at the difficult hurdles anyone faces in trying to escape the cycle, resulting in generational poverty, as the curse of being poor is passed down from one generation to another.

Here are some of the devastating truths I found, which cast hundreds of thousands of Baltimore residents and many millions around the nation into a poverty trap that is almost impossible to escape unless something is done to help them get out.

The Effects of Poverty on the Development of Children

One enduring effect of poverty is on the development of children. From their early childhood, both their health and brain development are hurt, by a poor education in deteriorating schools, poor nutrition, and the pervasive threat of danger in the streets. So, they do not develop many of the skills other children in more affluent areas develop naturally.

An example of this is shown in a groundbreaking study conducted by Johns Hopkins University researchers. They followed nearly eight hundred Baltimore children for a quarter of a century to see how their early development affected their later life—and the results were shocking as the way poverty stunted their lives. As sociologist Karl Alexander, who led the study, reported in *The Long Shadow: Family Background, Disadvantaged Urban Youth, and the Transition to Adulthood*: "A family's resources and the doors they open cast a long shadow over children's life trajectories." And for children growing up in poverty, this was a very long, very dark shadow.[12]

The researchers began their study in 1982, when the children entered first grade, and they followed the children's journey through life until they were twenty-eight or twenty-nine years old, focusing on those in the most disadvantaged settings. The researchers found that when these people were nearly thirty years old, almost half were in the same socioeconomic status as their parents. "The poor stayed poor; those better off remained better off." In fact, only thirty-three children moved from the lower income bracket of their birth to a higher income bracket. But if family background had no bearing on their achievement in life, almost seventy would be expected to move ahead. By contrast, among those who started out in a well-off family, only nineteen dropped down to a low-income bracket.

Some of the researchers' findings showed even more dramatically the daunting odds that children of poverty, especially black children, face.

Almost none of the children from poor families made it through college. At twenty-eight, only 4 percent of the children of poverty had a college degree, compared to 45 percent of the children from higher-income families, who were over ten times as likely to go to college.

Even if they completed college, only 15 percent of the black men from low-income families were working in the construction trades and industrial crafts, compared to 45 percent of the white men from the same background.

Although both white and black men from lower-income families earned less than white men, the disadvantages were even worse for black women. They not only had lower incomes, but "they were less likely than whites to be in stable family unions, and so were less likely to benefit from a spouse's earnings."

How Poverty Can Damage the Child's Brain

One of the most amazing findings from this research, which made me sick to my stomach, is that growing up poor stunts the brains of young children. It actually affects the structures underlying higher-level cognition—like will power, emotional self-control, and decision-making—when the cerebral cortex develops.[13]

Pat Levitt, a developmental neuroscientist at Children's Hospital in Los Angeles, discovered that the conditions that often occur with poverty—like substandard housing, noise, overcrowding, family turmoil, separation from parents, exposure to violence, to name a few—"can be toxic to the developing brain, just like drug or alcohol abuse." These conditions lead the body to release hormones like cortisol, produced in the adrenal cortex. While a burst of cortisol can help a person better respond to a difficult challenge—it is part of the fight-or-flight response—over a long term, an excess of cortisol can harm the brain. For example, when a pregnant woman has a build-up of cortisol, it can be transferred to the fetus through the placenta, where it may affect the brain's circuitry. When this child grows up, he or she may have a higher level of cortisol, which continues to undermine the brain's development.

Still other research shows this potential devastation on the brains of young children. A study done by researchers from nine hospitals and universities published in the March 2015 issue of Nature Neuroscience[14] took DNA samples from over a thousand children, performed MRI scans of their brains and obtained data on the income level and educational background of the children's families. They then tested the children in reading ability, memory, and other skills.

The dramatic results highlighted why it is so important to start early to overcome the effects of poverty. As the researchers found, the children from the lowest income homes had up to 6 percent less brain surface area and a smaller hippocampus—the center in the brain that stores memories—than the children from high-income families. Moreover, they found that at the very bottom of the income spectrum small increases in family earnings could mean larger brains, leading them to conclude that "wealth can't necessarily buy a better brain, but deprivation can result in a weakened one."

This reduced brain size can lead to major long-term behavioral and cognitive difficulties. In another study, described by Madeline Ostrander, "What Poverty Does to the Young Brain," neuroscientists at four universities scanned the brains of a group of young adults, now twenty-four, and found that those who had lived in poverty at nine-years old had more active centers of negative emotions, whereas the areas that could restrain these emotions were quieter. Still other studies have shown that stress in childhood makes people prone to depression, heart disease, and addiction as adults.[15]

Thus we see, "poverty perpetuates poverty, generation after generation, by acting on the brain." This is why The National Scientific Council has been prodding policymakers to initiate or back measures that break the poverty cycle, which begins before birth, by, for instance, providing better prenatal and pediatric care to low-income moms and extending preschool to poor children. Additionally, the researchers advocate changing the laws that criminalize drug abuse during pregnancy, since "arrest and incarceration can also trigger the 'maternal stress response system,' which can damage the developing [fetal] brain."

I agree that such strategies are needed, now that we know the damage poverty can do to children. Not only do these children face a devastating and demoralizing lifestyle, but the very structures of their brains are damaged in their early years, even before they are born. These contribute to their struggles later, like learning and staying in school, because these damages interfere with their ability to acquire knowledge and remember what they are taught.

Disturbing Facts about Poverty in Baltimore

So, how extensive is poverty in Baltimore? What are the effects on the individual's life? To find out, I looked at some articles and US Census data describing the nature of this problem in Baltimore. This is what I found from the census data, which shows the extent of poverty in Baltimore compared to Maryland as a whole:[16]

At about 623,000 residents, Baltimore city represents about 10 percent of Maryland's 5.98 million residents, although compared to the state, Baltimore has shown little growth—only 0.3 percent compared to 3.5 percent for the state. Perhaps one reason for its slower growth is its extensive poverty, leading many residents to pull up stakes when they can. In other ways, Baltimore's population is comparable to Maryland's as a whole, since about 21 to 23 percent of the population in both areas is under the age of eighteen, 12 to 13 percent are sixty-five or older, and females represent 52 to 53 percent of the population.

However, the demographics and the poverty statistics of the city compared to the state are starkly different. They show how Baltimore has become a center for largely African-American poverty. As of 2013, the black population in Baltimore was 63 percent, compared to 30 percent in the state, while the white alone population was 60 percent in the state, only 32 percent in Baltimore. The other major difference is in the Asian and Hispanic populations. In Baltimore, Asians are about 3 percent of the population; in the state, about twice as much at 6 percent. As for Hispanics, about 4.6 percent are in the city, about 9 percent in the state.

These statistics along with income differences show the relationship between a larger black population and poverty. While the per capita income for 2009 to 2013 was $24,750 for Baltimore city, it was $36,354 for Maryland as a whole, and the median Baltimore household income was $41,385 versus $73,538 for the state—nearly 78 percent higher.

As you might expect, one reason for these stark differences is just how many of Baltimore's residents—largely black—below the poverty line. As the census data shows, between 2009 and 2013, 23.8 percent of the population was below the poverty line, compared to 9.8 percent statewide. These differences show up in the housing data too. For example:

The homeownership rate in Baltimore was 48.3 percent, compared to 67.6 percent in the state.

The median value of owner-occupied housing units was $158,000 in Baltimore, but nearly double that— $293,000—in the rest of the state.

The percent of housing in multi-unit structures—usually rental properties, like apartment buildings—was 32.4 percent in Baltimore, only 25.5 percent in the state.

The differences are shown in the educational data, too. During this same time, the percentage of those twenty-five and older with a bachelor's degree was only 27 percent in Baltimore, compared to 37 percent in Maryland as a whole. And since a college degree is a ticket to most good jobs, these percentage differences are another measure of how the largely black population in Baltimore has fallen behind.

Still other data show the effects of this high level of poverty, like the statistics cited in an article by Sarah Gray in "Six Shocking Facts About Poverty in Baltimore."[17]

84 percent of Baltimore's public school students are poor enough that they qualify for a free or reduced-price school lunch.

Baltimore teenagers feel worse about their situation than teens in New Delhi and Ibadan, Nigeria, according to a 2014 Johns Hopkins University's "Well-Being of Adolescents in Vulnerable Environments" study. The researchers found, after interviewing 2,400 teens ages fifteen to nineteen in New Delhi, Johannesburg, Shanghai, and Ibadan, Nigeria, the teens in Johannesburg and Baltimore felt the worst about their current circumstances. Also, they found that teens from these two cities experienced the most severe health consequences, reflected in "high rates of mental health problems, substance use, sexual experience and pregnancy, and sexual violence."[18]

Poverty rates have long been a problem in Baltimore, based on a study from 1970 to 2010, which found that poverty in the city increased from thirty-eight poor neighborhoods in 1970 to fifty-five neighborhoods in 2010. At the same time, many high-poverty neighborhoods experienced a huge drop in population, because of people moving because conditions were so bad. For example, in one Baltimore census track, the poverty rate fell from 30 percent in 1970 to less than fifteen percent in 2010, because many people who were impoverished moved someplace else.

Baltimore is one of the top cities to receive food stamps, according to a Business Insider article. Between 2007 and 2009, 24 percent of the residents were using food stamp benefits and 42 percent of the children were on food stamps.

In Freddie Gray's neighborhood, about 52 percent of the residents between the ages of sixteen and sixty-four were unemployed and one third of the buildings were vacant between 2008 and 2012

Perhaps a key reason for the daunting poverty statistics is that Baltimore, which used to be a hub for the steel industry, lost more than a hundred thousand manufacturing jobs between 1950 and 1995. And the city never really recovered from those losses.

Unfortunately, once poverty sets in, it creates a cycle. Since children raised in these circumstances are affected even from birth, as their brains develop, so they are disadvantaged from the get-go.

The Effects of Poverty

Poverty hurts not only the poor, but society as a whole. Consider the eruption of violence in Baltimore. Society suffers in multiple ways, like the loss of the contribution an impoverished individual might have made and the cost of their crimes when they seek illegal income. It also suffers when the impoverished individual, in desperation, commits crimes or violence, like burning down stores and cars, maybe striking back at what they see as an unjust society. Plus there's the cost of incarcerating millions of offenders who might not be in that situation but for growing up poor. It is a vicious cycle that has become increasingly vicious, as reflected in what happened in Baltimore.

Thus, after looking at the grim statistics, I wanted to look deeper into the effects of poverty. Reading much of this information made my stomach turn. I was often nauseated by the information many of our leaders and decision-makers should be referring to when making important decisions regarding our communities.

I read an article titled "Baltimore Riots 2015: City Residents' Struggle Under Poverty, Income Inequality, and Mass Incarceration Predates Freddie Gray Unrest" by Howard Koplowitz, a reporter with the *International Business Times*. This piece was eye-opening to say the least. It describes how Freddie Gray was one of four hundred people from the area who were jailed or imprisoned in only a few months because of the economic struggles that affected many residents.[19]

As Koplowitz describes, a key reason the riots erupted is that "many residents feel frustration over the lack of opportunity and mobility—factors that could point people like Gray to lives of crime and poverty." Moreover, not only have there been many years of socioeconomic disparity, but the city has done little to deal with the systemic issues that cause the "cycle of poverty, criminality, and low educational attainment."[20]

Unfortunately, another effect of poverty is a high incarceration rate and high costs to the city that come with this. Incredibly, a third of Maryland residents in state prison are from Baltimore, though the city has only about 10 percent of the state population, accordingly to the Justice Policy Institute.[21]

The costs to the state are astronomical. The taxpayers in Maryland spend approximately $288 million a year to incarcerate nearly 7,800 people from Baltimore. But if just half of these people were working, the cost would be half as much, while the taxes collected—if they were each earning, say, $30,000 a year—would be in the millions each year. It's a huge savings, and thousands of people would become productive members of society instead of criminals. But for now, that isn't the reality for Baltimore. Instead, obtaining employment, housing, and treatment for health problems, and establishing positive social networks is more difficult for low-income Baltimore residents generally, and even more difficult for those coming out of jail.

The statistics also show that poverty was especially hard on the black youth of Baltimore, as Charles D. Ellison points out in "Baltimore's Slow Burn of Poverty and Hopelessness" Baltimore's official 8.4 percent unemployment rate, almost double the national average, is even worse for black men—and especially for black youth. In Sandtown-Winchester, where Freddie lived before his arrest, 27 percent of black males from ages sixteen to sixty-four were unemployed in 1970. But that figure rose to 42 percent in 2012, whereas only 22 percent of their white counterparts were unemployed that same year, according to a University of Wisconsin-Milwaukee multi-city study. And the unemployment rate for Baltimore's black youth was 16.1 percent, two percentage points above the average youth unemployment rate, and "almost triple the overall national jobless rate."[22]

Making matters worse, the vast majority of whites in Baltimore don't recognize that racial discrimination is contributes to the problem. As Ellison notes, 70 percent of whites considered racial discrimination in their local communities a nonproblem.[23]

Yet, racial discrimination is clearly a factor, since the city's black poverty rate, at just under 24 percent, is much higher than the state's black poverty rate of 14 percent.[24] In fact, poverty in certain neighborhoods has gone up, according to a City Observatory Report, since fifty-five areas are considered "high poverty."

As Ellison notes, and as I often see myself on the streets. Places like West Baltimore's Sandtown-Winchester neighborhood, where Freddie lived, are tinderboxes full of people with nothing to lose. Gentrification displaces the poor while city leaders dress the Inner Harbor and downtown with lavish venues after spending money they could never find for the people who need it the most.

The irony is that Baltimore is a relatively affluent city, ranking seventh in the nation among thirty-five metro areas, according to a Brookings Institute report, since it has a per capita income of $54,457. Only San Jose, San Francisco-Oakland, Boston, Washington, DC, New York, and Seattle rank above it.[25]

Baltimore also has a significant middle class, and ranks second in the black median household income among these cities, with a black median household income of $47,898. It is only outranked by Washington, DC. Plus, it has a significant number of jobs and residents in its downtown area, since it ranks ninth among twenty-five major metro areas in population and twelfth in the number of jobs—123,879 in 2014, according to the State of Town Report 2015, published by the Downtown Partnership of Baltimore.

Yet, in contrast to this image of a thriving affluent city is the other Baltimore, the one of the poor in certain areas west and east of downtown, which are largely black. In this case, Baltimore City ranked twelfth among thirty-five metro areas with the largest black populations, and in the poorest districts, 75 percent or more of the population was African-American. Thus, as the report concludes, "black residents of Baltimore City fare much worse than white residents on key economic measures."[26]

The results are devastating, as the report notes:

> Within the city of Baltimore, deep divisions exist by race and place. Neighborhoods just to the west and east of downtown Baltimore, including Sandtown-Winchester and extending out into suburban Baltimore County, exhibit very high rates of poverty. Those neighborhoods are predominantly black, reflecting a long history of explicit and implicit policies in the region that yielded high levels of racial and economic segregation. The racial isolation and poverty concentration help account for stark differences between Baltimore's black and white populations in key economic outcomes like education, employment, and child poverty.

Yet, in spite of this grim description of the divide in Baltimore, some cities have higher poverty and lower employment among blacks than Baltimore, so it might only be a matter of time before these cities erupt in violence too. Some of the cities with the largest black populations as of 2013—San Antonio, Hartford, Lexington, Portsmouth (Virginia), Paterson (New Jersey), Houston, Jersey City, Savannah, St. Petersburg,

Beaumont (Texas), Newport News, and Oakland—also have the largest poor black populations.

Some of these cities have already experienced eruptions. Oakland suffered protests, looting, and the burning of cars and businesses throughout downtown. These were in sympathy to the protests in Ferguson after the killing of Michael Brown. The protests and riots in Baltimore may readily spread to other cities that have high poverty especially affecting blacks. What happened in Baltimore might be the canary in the mine, reminding the nation of the dangers that await if this cycle of poverty and pain continues.

Other Negative Effects of Poverty on Children and Teens

As I continued my research on poverty in Baltimore, I found still other ways in which it hurt the opportunities and living conditions of everyone, especially children and teens.

As described by Jonah Goldberg in "To Break the Cycle of Poverty in Baltimore, Fix the Culture of Poverty," living in poverty limits one's earning ability, according to new studies by Harvard economist Raj Chetty and his associates. In one study, Chetty found that the sooner kids got out of impoverished neighborhoods, the better they did in life and the more they earned. They were "much more likely to go to college and earn more." He estimated that giving kids, who were an average of 8 years old in his study, a voucher to move into a more prosperous area would increase their lifetime earnings by about $302,000.

And girls who received these vouchers were 26 percent less likely to end up as single mothers.

Then, when Chetty and other colleagues looked at the earnings data for five million US families over a seventeen-year period, they found that neighborhoods significantly shape the outcomes for children because of better schools, communities, neighbors, local amenities, economic opportunities, and social norms. Inside impoverished communities, poor kids suffer a deficit in these compared to kids in wealthier communities.[27]

And these factors influence each other. They are like weights added to an individual already trying to hold up too much. Eventually the weight becomes too much and the person collapses.

When Chetty calculated the effects of growing up in a culture of poverty, he found that every extra year of childhood living in the worst areas of Baltimore reduced the earnings of a low-income boy by 1.39 percent.[28] So, if you add that up over the years of childhood—say, twenty years, until a boy turns twenty-one— that's 27.8 percent reduced earnings for a boy growing up in poverty. And for a boy who experiences further negative factors because of poverty, the outcome can be even worse.

It's a conclusion echoed by Nathaniel Hendren, a Harvard economist, who worked with Chetty on researching the role geography plays in shaping a child's chances of future success. As reported by Emily Badger in a *Washington Post* article, Baltimore is at the bottom of the ladder for percentage loss in income because of growing up poor, and it's especially bad for low-income boys. There is a loss of 17.3 percent for all children in Baltimore, but the loss is 27.9 percent for boys, and it's only 5.4 percent for girls.[29]

Unfortunately, growing up in poverty is like a life sentence that one cannot escape because it limits social mobility, so the sooner families can move out, the better their children will do, according to Chetty, Hendren, and Lawrence Katz. As they all found, the places in America with the most economic mobility for poor kids are not generally where blacks live. That's because, as Chetty notes:

> ...places with larger African-American populations have a lot of other disadvantages. They tend to be much more segregated. They tend to have less investment in things like public schools, and this lack of investment has adverse effects on both African-Americans and whites.[30]

For example, Chetty and his team found that the counties with the worst social mobility, like Baltimore City and Wayne County in Detroit, had the largest black populations, while those with the greatest social mobility for the poor had few blacks, like Dupage County in suburban Chicago.

Still other research has shown that poverty affects the well-being of adolescents and young children. The WAVE study (Well-Being of Adolescents in Vulnerable Environments)[31] looked at young people fifteen to nineteen living in the poorest neighborhoods of some of the world's largest cities. It chose Baltimore as one of five cities, since it was the home base of one of the participating institutions, the Johns Hopkins Bloomberg School of Public Health. The researchers recognized that youth living in impoverished urban areas are more vulnerable than their more well-to-do counterparts to several damaging factors. They have health challenges because of dirty and crowded physical environments; less education and fewer job opportunities; frequent encounters with violence, crime, and drugs; often dangerous working conditions; and limited health services, especially for teens. The team wanted to document these problems systemically and look at the factors associated with poorer and better health to identify potential ways to improve the well-being of the youth.[32]

Among other things, the WAVE team found that the youth from Baltimore and Johannesburg gave their communities the lowest ratings, even though, ironically, the Baltimore neighborhood is located in a wealthy country. Moreover, the researchers found that direct measures of social capital are associated with self-reported health. In other words, growing up poor is bad for your health, besides contributing to the many other problems that go along with being poor.

Additionally, the researchers found that the teens in economically distressed areas had higher levels of self-reported depression, post-traumatic stress, and thoughts of suicide. In Baltimore, more than a quarter of the teens had a high level of at least one of these symptoms. Although having a caring female adult in the home and feeling connected to their neighborhood were positively associated with hope and these teens were less likely to suffer depression or post-traumatic stress.

The researchers also found substance abuse common in teens in poor areas; about two-thirds of the teens reported they had used at least one substance during their life. Most commonly the Baltimore teens used marijuana (55 percent) and alcohol (52 percent).[33] They also found that the level of sexual experience was much higher in Baltimore and Johannesburg, where the majority of youth reported a sexual experience. Pregnancy was especially common in Baltimore, where half of the girls reported a pregnancy—often associated with being out of school and experiencing more community violence.[34]

Finally, the researchers looking at sexual and partner violence found that about 25 percent of the women reported sexual violence with an intimate partner in both cities, and over 10 percent of the girls experienced nonpartner sexual violence. Additionally, the researchers found that both types of sexual violence are associated with poor sexual and reproductive health, mental health, and self-rated health. Given these findings, the researchers concluded that this level of sexual violence suggested that "disadvantaged urban environments serve as incubators of gender-based violence risk for young women."

The researchers further found that adolescents in Baltimore and Johannesburg experienced the most severe consequences, since they had high rates of mental health problems, substance use, sexual experience, pregnancy, and sexual violence.

Additionally, they rated their community very poorly overall because of the rundown environment and atmosphere of violence they confronted every day. The researchers concluded that these communities were the most toxic, though the teens in the other cities studied also had high levels of mental health problems and substance use compared to the general population. These conditions set the stage for chronic problems later in life.

Such findings are probably well-known to the people living in low-income neighborhoods and struggling with poverty every day. Still, it is helpful when researchers can report these findings because it gives the problem legitimacy. Then, policymakers and legislators can point to these authoritative sources to urge that something be done to address poverty.

In a way, the protests and riots in Baltimore were like the research reports of academics drawing attention to the problem and calling for a solution to the day-to-day frustrations of poverty and their devastating effects from childhood through adolescence to adulthood. But these residents don't have the same kind of platform or authority as the researchers to point out the reality of what they see around them every day. So for them, the protests and riots are their brush, painting a picture of the damaging conditions they experience every day. They are a way to express their anger on the canvas of our city and to call out to the rest of society to recognize and act to fix it.

How Baltimore Can Serve as an Example

As I learned more about the ravages of poverty, I thought about how these lessons could be applied to the rest of our nation, since poverty is rampant in other major cities as well. Baltimore may have erupted—as did Ferguson, Staten Island, and elsewhere in response to black killings by police officers— but that encounter is only an indicator of the other damages of poverty, especially as experienced by blacks in the inner city.

These eruptions are the tip of an iceberg, which will show itself to be even more dangerous.

The problems of poverty are everywhere. The PovertyUSA website points out that more than forty-six million Americans live in poverty, while the PovertyUSA anti-poverty program, organized by US Catholic bishops through the Catholic Campaign for Human Development, is designed to educate and promote understanding about poverty and its root causes.

Unfortunately, poverty has long been with us. Back in the 1960s, Michael Harrington, the contributing editor of Dissent and author of *The Other America: Poverty in the United States,* estimated that forty to fifty million Americans, about one-quarter of the population, lived in poverty, where they were "hard put to get the mere necessities, beginning with enough to eat."[35]

Now we seem to be living in a kind of time-warp: the same number of Americans are among us, though instead of being buried in rural outposts like Appalachia, they are sequestered in the low-income, high-crime inner city neighborhoods. Back then, the invisible poor were primarily farmers, migratory farm works, and unskilled, unorganized workers in service jobs in hotels, restaurants, hospitals, and laundries. They lived in areas where poverty was endemic, like in the rural south or in West Virginia after the closing of the coal mines and steel plants. Back then the poor also included African-Americans, who were about a fourth of the total poor—the alcoholic derelicts on skid row in the big cities, hillbillies from the South who migrated to Midwestern cities to find better jobs, and about half of the country's senior citizens.[36]

Thinking back to the early 1960s when Harrington was writing, I noticed that most of the previously poor groups disappeared from the landscape, because of changing technologies and economic conditions that uprooted the farmers and replaced a rural backwater South with new urbanized metropolises. Today, African-Americans lead the nation in percentage of poor by race, but like the previous generations of poor, we too have become invisible, in part because we are still a minority. As Dwight MacDonald points out in "Our Invisible Poor" in the 1963 New Yorker, "That mass poverty can persist despite this rise to affluence is hard to believe."[37]

Back then he was referring to the affluence of the middle class that increased from 13 percent of all families to a near majority (47 percent) as of 1963. But now, while the middle class has been disappearing, this affluence is concentrated among the top 1 to 10 percent of the population, according to various calculations.

However, the numbers are determined, many of the main characteristics of poverty are still with us today. For example, then and now, the poor suffer from more obesity because they eat cheap carbohydrates with little nutritional value and don't exercise as much—simply because good food is so much more expensive. Additionally, the costs of poverty spread through society, then as now. As MacDonald notes:

> Every citizen has a right to become or remain part of our society because if this right is denied, as it is in the case of at least one-fourth of our citizens, it impoverishes us all…Nobody starves, but who can measure the starvation, not to be calculated by daily intake of proteins and

calories that reduces life for many of our poor to a long vestibule to death? Nobody starves, but every fourth citizen rubs along on a standard of living that is below…"the minimal levels of health, housing, food, and education that our present stage of scientific knowledge specifies as necessary for life as it is now lived in the United States."[38] Nobody starves, but a fourth of us are excluded from the common social existence. Not to be able to afford a movie or a glass of beer is a kind of starvation—if everybody else can.

These words were written over fifty years ago, in 1963. But they still resonate today because we still suffer from "the persistence of mass poverty in a prosperous country." Until every citizen can feel he or she can live above the poverty line and feel included as a party of the rest of the country, the "shame of the Other America will continue."

I'll talk later about what we should do about this gaping wound in our country—the one-quarter or more of our population in Baltimore and other cities around America that still struggle with poverty and the devastation it brings to the community. But for now, a first step is to become aware of the depth of the problem. Then we can figure out a solution. The protests and riots following Freddie Gray's death, much like that in other cities after incidents of police brutality and racial injustice, have made us aware of the extent of the problem and the tragedy of wasted lives in so many cities. The next step will be to follow up on this awareness with action, as I'll discuss in future chapters.

CHAPTER 6
VOICES IN THE CITY

The voices in Baltimore are unique and as diverse as anywhere else in the world. Whether it's the taxi driver who grew up in Afghanistan, the kid from the West side who spends his entire day on the basketball court, or the fifty-five-year-old waitress who works sixty hours a week, everyone has a voice and everyone has an opinion. In Baltimore many of us see the world in a different light based on our own experiences and own belief system. Whether it's where to find the best crab cakes, who's the best football linebacker ever, or who's responsible for Freddie Gray's death, we all see things in a different way. In regards to the uprising in Baltimore and the Freddie Gray case the same rules apply.

So now, from that perspective, I wanted to look at Baltimore's potential recovery and growth. And again I spoke with David Nevins to get another perspective on how Baltimore might develop in the future. What was Baltimore's outlook and how can we overcome the problems of the past to move toward greatness?

Baltimore's Potential to Become a Great City

David, you have often talked about how Baltimore has the potential to be a great leading city.

Yes, if you look at what makes a city great, like some of the great cities in America like New York, Chicago, and San Francisco—one factor is geography. In the case of Baltimore, we have a great location going for us too. We're right on the Interstate 95 corridor for easy freeway access, and we're on the beautiful Chesapeake Bay and minutes to the Atlantic Ocean.

Also, we have world-class educational institutions, like Johns Hopkins University, and one of the best healthcare systems in the world, not only on the East Coast and in the United States, but in the world. Another key is that we have a population, based on my experience, which is composed of very good, hardworking people.

Looking back post–Freddie Gray, it seems to me that the key thing we lack is that not all of our population has the same opportunities—but we can fix that. You and I have a great opportunity to experience the best Baltimore has to offer. We're able to eat in the best restaurants in the city. I've walked the harbor with my wife, kids, and friends. I walk through Fells Point, historic neighborhoods, Federal Hill. We can experience Baltimore as a great place to raise a family. And we can quickly travel wherever we want. We can be in New York City in two hours. We can be in Washington, DC, the nation's capital, in forty-five minutes. So Baltimore has it all for me and for you.

The Barriers for Many in Baltimore

Yet, when we talk about how Baltimore doesn't have it all for everybody, but can become a possibility for everyone, there are barriers in place to creating a divided Baltimore and many people don't understand both sides. So, David, how do we begin to have that conversation on how to understand the plight of both sides? How do we reach out to the haves, have-nots, and everybody else in the middle to address the plight of Baltimore?

The way to fix things is so simple and so complicated at the same time. While I am not trying to discredit the viewpoint of my upper-middle-class white suburban golf buddies, I think it's fair to say that when suburbanites in general think of this situation, they immediately think, "This is easily fixed." And they suggest quick fixes and cosmetic changes. For example, they say that the kids who are in school need to make sure they go there and do the homework they are assigned. After all, that's what the successful kids did when I went to school. I got home and did two or three hours' worth of homework, before my parents would let me out to play football or catch in the yard or in the street. What they don't understand are the social issues affecting these families. That's the part they are missing, and it's a big part. They don't understand the issues of poverty and how this harms black families. It's foreign to them. They don't get it.

So, in their simplified view of the world held by those in suburbia, they believe people just have to behave in a certain way, do certain things and live happily ever after. But if they don't conform that way, that's their problem. So, I think it's a pretty widespread and prevalent view among those in suburbia that this problem is self-inflicted. I'm not saying this is correct, but that's one commonly held view. Some of my white friends just don't get it when it comes to these issues. I won't say they're racist but I would say that many of them are ignorant to these issues.

The Perspective of the Poor in Urban America

What do you think might be done to change this viewpoint and overcoming these challenges, David?

One thing that helps is for everybody to recognize that there are challenges and discuss what to do about them. For example, at the Center Club we had a couple speakers recently on this issue with about a hundred attendees, centered around Freddie Gray, the protests, how this happened, and how to fix Baltimore.

One of the speakers crystallized the whole situation in a few words when he said, "Despair knows no etiquette." He went on to explain that we're speaking from our world and perspective when we say: "Lift yourself up by your boot straps, educate yourself, work hard, and live life happily ever after." But when you look at this situation from another perspective, it is not that easy—or realistic.

This gentleman was speaking from this perspective of someone who lives in the world where folks are born into poverty. Many of them have lead paint in their tiny apartments. They have no air conditioning. The schools are terrible. Their hope is nonexistent. The mentors of young children are their young mothers, who have no sufficient life experience yet to be mentors. Many of the fathers are gone. The opportunity to earn a living is limited or nonexistent. For us to think that per motivation alone would change their situation is ridiculous.

For example, in my case, when I was a kid, I earned a living delivering newspapers and mowing lawns. But for these kids, there are no more newspapers to be delivered. There are no lawns to be mowed. There's an occasional McDonald's restaurant that is an employer of last resort. Then, if you can live past your youth, there are no jobs anywhere in your community that will deliver that middle class life that we all apparently seek. Better-paying factory jobs are gone too. Many years ago, the Bethlehem Steel Corporation was the largest employer in Baltimore. Today they employ zero folks. The local factory is no more. It's boarded up.

So, the urban poor live in a completely different world. My biggest problem when I go home tonight is to discuss with my wife what we are going to have for dinner, and if we don't have anything in the freezer, what restaurant are we going to go to and can we get a reservation. That's not the discussion taking place in urban, poor America. Rather, though many don't realize it, though some do, many thousands and thousands of young people and their parents live their lives in despair. Their lives, for the most part, are without hope, without a future. Then, if that's the case, apparently at some point a trigger occurs, as in the case of Freddie Gray, and the person says to himself, "I've got nothing to lose." So, he goes out to commit a crime, or in the case of Freddie Gray, he carries a switchblade, which gets him arrested, put in the back of a police van, put in jail, or whatever happens next.

Solving the Have-Have-Not Problem

But haven't we had many triggers over the years, David? Haven't we had many situations similar to Freddie Gray? Why now?

I think the eruption in Baltimore happened now because of a combination of factors, a perfect storm, if you will. A lot of our politicians and leaders are beginning to talk about this. For any number of reasons, over the last couple of decades, those of us who live in the upper middle class and upper class have thrived, while those who don't have suffered.

The problem is that the gap between the haves and the have-nots is bigger than ever. This reminds me of a story about a good friend who was the customer service manager for a national company. One day, he had to go into a small town about an hour's drive from Baltimore, since, as a cost-saving move to make this company more profitable and more efficient, he had to shut down a small call center. This center employed about fifty people, mostly elderly women, each making less than $50,000 a year. Fifty times $50,000 is two and a half million dollars, so eliminating these positions, combined with rent for the call center building and a few other expenses, saved this Fortune 500 company three million dollars a year.

The shareholders would all go, "Great!" at this savings. Ironically, the very same week of this shutdown, the company board of directors awarded the company's two top officers bonuses of about thirty million dollars. So, the same week that the company is giving their very successful senior officers sixty million dollars, they're firing fifty people—each of whom made less than $50,000—to save three million dollars.

Now, if that's a good thing in America today, that's what I'm talking about when I say the gap between the haves and have-nots is becoming bigger than ever. That's fifty people without a job because of the shutdown. Perhaps this may sound naïve of me to say this, but couldn't these two top officers have survived with fifty-seven million dollars instead of sixty million? Couldn't these fifty people have kept their jobs?

Is that a disconnect or is that greed, David, since in America, part of the goal of capitalism is to make as much money as you can? Is that a disconnect in that these gentlemen didn't get the connection between the big bonuses paid to their top officers and the fifty unemployed individuals?

I think that's a terrific question, Kevin, and I think it's both. On the one hand, I wouldn't say these gentlemen didn't get it. My guess is that they probably weren't even aware of this decision to shut down this fifty person call center. That decision happened several layers beneath them. Then the company board of directors—made up of their friends and colleagues who were thinking, "If you scratch my back, I'll scratch yours"—said, "Let's award them with sixty million dollars" because the company is doing so well.

Somehow we have gotten to the point in this country where we have forgotten a key principle of society: that we really are our brother's keeper. We have to look after each other to make society work.

So, I think asking about that disconnect and greed is an important question. I'm generally not in favor of higher taxes, but there used to be much more charitable giving by the wealthy to the less fortunate in society. Today, charitable giving in this country is not at an all-time high. Say the folks who made sixty million dollars or more decided to give ten or twenty million dollars of it away to charities in urban America, that would probably be a good thing. Then all might be right again with the world. Those on the lowest rungs of society could be helped and feel more satisfied that they had opportunities and hope for the future.

But we have a society where everybody's trying to climb, climb, and climb, and then climb some more. It's greed, it's a lack of awareness, a disconnect, and all the other problems we talked about. Certainly, the most amazing thing to me is that we live in a society today where communication is so quick, immediate, plentiful, and comprehensive. Yet for someone in my position and in the seat of the executives that I just mentioned, our lives do not interact with the protesters and the looters of Baltimore. At least they haven't until today.

The first time in my lifetime in Baltimore that they interacted was because of Freddie Gray. They interacted because all of a sudden, there's a curfew, so I can't go to my favorite restaurant in downtown Baltimore because of that. Others have similarly been affected by not being able to do things they used to do. So, when I talk about the silver lining on this Freddie Gray incident, it is that we've all been educated and made much more aware of the disparities and the differences.

The solution to this is not simply to throw more money at the problem. The solution is not just for wealthy people to give more money to charity. What's needed is a comprehensive solution where urban blacks also must say, "We need to take on some responsibility. We need to take school more seriously. We need to help the government and the private sector. We need job opportunities and training programs, and we need companies throughout the country to stop manufacturing everything in Vietnam and India." So, we really need a more comprehensive solution that involves everyone at all levels of society working together.

When we talk about a comprehensive approach that involves everyone coming together, there's always a need for leadership. So, David, what do you see as the impact of leadership on this bridge-building effort here in Baltimore in the last thirty years? You indicated when you first came to Baltimore in 1972 that there was an unofficial self-imposed segregation. But forty years later it still exists. So, how do we bridge that gap to bring us together to work on this problem?

Over the years we've had some good leaders and some not-so-good leaders, but neither the good leaders nor the bad leaders have fixed this problem. We argue over whether the police force should operate with zero tolerance or should operate as in New York City with apparently more tolerance. I don't know the answer to these questions, but we need to answer them to move ourselves out of this have-and-have-not dilemma we face.

Clearly, if you have money, whether you're white or black, if you live in Guilford, Roland Park, or other nice communities, like Fells Point, Canton, or Federal Hill, or in newer communities like Harbor East, you're going to say the leadership is doing a pretty good job. That's because you have these fabulous luxury apartments, condos, or multimillion dollar townhouses or other luxurious living accommodations. But the problem is we are not one Baltimore at the moment.

Overcoming the Great Divide

But will we ever be one Baltimore, David?

Whether we will ever become one Baltimore depends, of course, on one's definition of "One Baltimore." I like to use the economic model to analyze the situation. If I were to own a million-dollar waterfront condo in Baltimore, it is not worth as much today as it was the day before Freddie Gray died. It is worth less. Why is it worth less? Because there's less demand to live in the city of Baltimore right now. There's less demand to live around the harbor because people now see how quickly an uprising can occur or a situation can affect their well-being. If I were to live in one of those places, I think it's time for us to rec-ognize that my physical and financial well-being are tied to the well-being of the poor communities, which live in blight, just six, eight, ten, twenty blocks away.

The One Baltimore theme is a good one to use in seeking a solution. The goal of one Baltimore doesn't mean that we will become an integrated city and that everybody will live in everybody else's neighborhood. It does mean that if we don't figure out how to share the wealth, how to live peaceably with one another, and how to respect one another, we will be a divided city. In my view, I think much of this division has been caused by the lack of respect between the community and the police. I'm not saying which caused which, because this goes back to the chicken-and-the-egg question. It doesn't matter which came first. Rather, if we can figure out how to show respect and decency, share jobs, and not make thirty million dollars but make twenty-eight million so we let the other folks keep their jobs and earn a middle-class living, then I think we can create one Baltimore—and even one nation.

So how do we get from here to there, David? For example, if a guy asks me to describe life on the moon, I couldn't describe it, because I've never been to the moon. I couldn't tell you what it looks like or, most importantly, what it feels like. So when we use the term "golf buddies" and "upper middle class" to describe individuals on the "have" side of the equation, how do we get those individuals to really understand the plight of a person in poverty to better understand their needs? There's an obvious disconnect in the communication and understanding between the two groups. But there's also a disconnect in how we got here in the first place.

In my mind, David, the only way we can come up with a plan to get out is to fully understand each other. This is like going to the doctor to get a diagnosis for an illness, but the doctor can't diagnose the illness, so he can't come up with a cure or solution. How do we get both sides, not just golf

buddies, but the guys in the hood, on the corner, the guys making twelve dollars an hour and barely making it—how do we get both sides to better understand each other so that collectively we can come together with a solution? Obviously, the solutions that we tried to impose over the last twenty-five or thirty years in Baltimore haven't worked. Now, how do we make sure that collectively we understand each other, so that we can move Baltimore forward?

To answer your question, Kevin, the good news is that we understand more today than we did a couple of months ago before the Freddie Gray incident. My golf buddies understand more today than they did then, and vice-versa in the lower-income communities. That's the good news.

But moving past that understanding—because this effort is still in its infancy—is the big question. At least we know things that didn't work. For example, if you go back to the days of busing, the thinking was, "We're going to take kids in the urban area and bus them to suburban schools, where they're going to get good educations." But that didn't work. It just cost a lot of money, disrupted communities, and the kids generally didn't improve in their new schools. In fact, I think it's fair to say that the billions and billions of dollars spent in the last fifty years on different social programs, including the current food stamp program and the current welfare program, haven't seemed to move the needle as far as we would have liked.

It would be nice if our leaders, whatever their party—Democrats, Republicans, Independents, liberals, or conservatives—recognized that no one's blaming anybody. But whatever we've been doing so far hasn't worked. It's time for a new plan.

Taking Responsibility

But David, what about the question of responsibility in the black community? And whose fault is it that today, in 2015, we're still talking about a race divide, unemployment, and social programs that haven't worked? Who's responsible and at fault for that? Baltimore has been a Democratic city for decades, where the mayor and majority of city council have been Democrats. When we talk about the black community taking responsibility, where's the responsibility of our leadership for the problems they haven't solved?

Kevin, I think the solution will only result if we all recognize that you can't point your finger in any single direction and assign a percentage of fault, like to say that 90 percent of it is the fault of liberal Democrats or President Johnson and the New Era. I don't think that's true and I don't think that's a winnable argument to attribute fault that way. I think we all clearly have to say it is our fault, with a capital O-U-R. It is a fault throughout American society of the last fifty years. So, I think the only way to solve the problem is if we all recognize that we have a part in it.

For example, to use my golf-buddy scenario for the suburban white middle- and upper-class, we don't understand why the leaders of the African-American community don't step up and challenge the African-American community to help itself out of this situation far more than they currently do. We don't understand it. At the same time, the situation is certainly not helped when those on Wall Street, most of whom are white, pocket tens of millions and sometimes billions of dollars, build their ten- and twenty-million-dollar mansions, and insulate their lives from all things bad or challenging. So I think the fault can lie across the board.

Kevin, I think the answer to what to do to deal with the problem is less about determining whose fault it is and more about how we can fix it.

How to Fix a Broken System

David, what about assessing the possibilities for loss or gain to determine what to do, as in deciding to go forward or not in a business venture? As an example, in Sandtown-Winchester, Mayor Kurt Schmoke had an ambitious plan to help that community years ago. Millions of dollars were spent to rebuild the Sandtown-Winchester area, but twenty years later, the place is just as bad as it was before millions of dollars were poured into it. Now, Kurt Schmoke, the former mayor, is a good man and also African-American, so I know his heart was in the right place. But were these bad ideas, bad plans, or bad leadership?

Yes, well put. My hope is that we get it right this time around. West Baltimore and Baltimore as a whole is fragile right now. We can't afford to mess this up.

So, are we missing something, David, when our leaders have to make these types of decisions about whether to invest in an area? We're in that situation right now, since Washington, DC, is planning to pour millions of dollars into efforts here in Baltimore. Are we going down the same road we went down twenty years ago when Mayor Schmoke attempted to help the west side? How can we make sure that we get this right?

Unless we spend the money differently going forward, there's no reason to expect that we will fix the problem this time around. I think that it requires a new approach. We need to make these fixes quickly in Baltimore, and in all of urban America. And it is especially critical that we figure out a way to educate our young people so that they can help themselves in order to work, earn a living, and advance as high as they want. If they're happy living in a one-bedroom apartment and earning $25,000 a year, that's a wonderful thing. But those who want to figure out how to earn $100,000 a year ought to be given that opportunity, because that can allow them to buy a house. For those who want to start and build their own business and earn several times that, we've got to figure out a path for these people to be able to do it.

David, education has to be a major piece of the solution, and that means both dealing with…the cost and the broken system of education. Today, America is about twelfth in the world when it comes to education systems. We're behind places like the Netherlands and Japan when it comes to a top-rated system. Not only is America falling behind, but the cost of college tuition is so high it creates a major barrier for many kids. The cost is so high that even when a student finishes school, they have so much debt that when they get a job, they can't pay it off. And there's no way to get rid of this

debt, even in a bankruptcy. Say I get a job making $69,000 a year but then I have $60,000 worth of college debt that will escalate with the interest rates over those years. So, the high cost of education doesn't make sense. The system is so broken. So, how do we fix these problems to start leveling out the playing field?

That's very true, Kevin. But we have to start acting now and quickly. First, as a nation, we have to say that we want this fixed, because we're not happy with being twelfth, tenth, or eighth, or even sixth worldwide in our educational system. This nation was built on our desire to be the best country on the face of the earth, with the best education system, the best healthcare system, the best quality of life, and so on, and we've lost it all. We are no longer number one. So, first off, we have to agree we want to fix the problem. And the only way to fix it is to overcome the great divide between the haves and the have-nots. For those who are history buffs, there is no nation that has survived long-term with the discrepancy that we have in the country today between the haves and the have-nots.

But do the haves even understand the barriers and obstacles holding down the have-nots?

No, Kevin. But I'd like to think that we understand it today a little better than we did before the Freddie Gray incident. So now, post–Freddie Gray, we have this greater understanding. Let's take the next twenty years in Baltimore and show America what a great city is all about. Let's lift our hundreds of thousands of citizens out of poverty. Let's make sure they're self-empowered to rise as high and as fast as they want to live the life that they want. The solution is not just about leading an equal life. It's also about having the opportunity to get wherever we want to go in life.

One place to start is with transforming the educational system. College tuition in America is outrageous. The value is no longer there. We don't need to pay fifty thousand dollars more or less to make sure our kids go to the colleges that have the fanciest gym, the fanciest stadiums. On the first page of college websites, they talk about the success of their football teams and who has the biggest, tallest, nicest rock climbing wall. That's not what fixing the educational system is about. It's not about the lure of sports and recreational activities. We have to return an educational system, both K-12 and post K-12, where it's affordable, there's value, and it leads to self-empowerment. It has to prepare the students for good jobs, so they can make enough to live at least a comfortable life, or more. We have to restore the American dream for the many people who have been left behind in this time of growing disparity.

• • • • • •

Some of David's views and opinions here may sound harsh or callous, but at the end of the day he speaks for a lot of people who share his view. To understand the riots in Baltimore, you have to understand the environment here. The problems in Baltimore didn't start yesterday. They've lingered for decades. And until we're on the same page about fixing them, they will continue for decades to come. Until the decision-makers here in this city can look every man, woman, and child in this city in the eyes and say, "I understand your plight," nothing will change.

CHAPTER 7
BREAKING THE CYCLE

Some major triggers leading to the uprising in Baltimore, as in other major cities, are the growing wealth disparity and the concentration of poverty in the inner cities, where the majority of residents are African American. But there are other underlying factors. A key factor is the transformation of the economy in the last few decades, which has moved jobs away from manufacturing. The main source of this transformation is globalization and the rise of the tech industry, creating some new jobs but increasing automation replacing skilled workers. Meanwhile, workers are not only displaced in Baltimore and other cities, but may be unable to find new jobs because they don't have the skills or training needed to adapt to different requirements in the new job market.

A vicious cycle is upon us, where changing economic and social conditions contributes to the loss of jobs and income, the decline of inner city areas, the flight of those who can afford to live in the suburbs, and the growing impoverishment of large swaths of the city where the residents are primarily African-Americans. In turn, these conditions contribute to poor health, shorter life spans, fewer educational opportunities, more gangs, drugs, and crime, and thus higher incarceration rates—largely for African-American offenders—and a generation of kids with stunted opportunities.

This pattern is stark in Baltimore, a former industrialized city that has experienced the fallout from globalization for decades, and those negative effects have ripped out the heart of Baltimore. So now, this ravaged Baltimore is searching for a new identity.

I have felt these problems keenly myself, since I grew up in Baltimore. I witnessed people drawn into the underground economy of drug-dealing as a way to survive and thrive at a time when the city had few legitimate opportunities. Unfortunately, that is still the reality today for many poor people caught in this cycle.

Thus, this chapter addresses factors contributing to this downward spiral and consider some ways to break the cycle.

Although many programs alleviate some of the symptoms— like through grants to families for housing or education—these programs largely treat the symptoms rather than the underlying disease. As a result, we need much deeper structural and institutional changes in Baltimore. I'll start by discussing the major factors at the bottom of this turbulent funnel that has torn through the city, leaving destruction in its wake. But then let's discuss some of the strategies that might help to break the cycle that fuels urban decline and decay.

Globalization and the Loss of Manufacturing Jobs

There's no way to get around it. While some economists have claimed that globalization has been good for creating new jobs, many think this is a myth used by corporate interests to justify their growing power and financial gain.

Numerous economists point to the harm of the global economy on domestic jobs, even though the growing global marketplace has been good for some. As Chad Stone, the chief economist at the Center on Budget and Policy Priorities, points out in a *US News* article, "How to Deal with Globalization's Job Losses," what's "good for the average American is not necessarily good for every American." On the one hand, globalization and technological changes have helped to increase living standards over the past decades. But on the other hand, particular kinds of workers, firms, and communities have experienced serious losses. Though the aggregate losses are smaller than aggregate gains, these losses have mostly hurt the less privileged segments of society, contributing to the growing divide between the rich and poor. A key reason for this increasing divergence is that wages have dropped outside of the manufacturing sector, so the average household earns much less now than in past decades, when adjusted for inflation.[39]

Some economists agree with Stone that low-cost imports from China mean domestic manufacturers cannot compete, and factories move overseas. While these lower-cost goods save consumers money, the competition means not only fewer jobs, but less money in the remaining jobs since manufacturing jobs had been a source of higher income for skilled and semiskilled laborers.

This decline in jobs has been especially true in Baltimore with the closing of the manufacturing plants at Sparrows Point and Bethlehem Steel, at one point a mainstay of the Baltimore economy. But with the loss of manufacturing jobs, the growing job sectors are service and retail, which pay less. In fact, the low wages in these sectors has contributed to the spread of strikes for higher wages, with some protests directed at Walmart and major fast-food chains like McDonald's, where typical wages are only nine or ten dollars an hour, barely above the current federal minimum wage of $7.25—but not a living wage.

The Permanent Loss of Jobs Because of Globalization

Recognizing that job loss is permanent flies in the face of what some economists claim—that outsourcing jobs increases employment and wages in the United States—a position advocated by Dartmouth economist Matthew Slaughter. This approach was even argued by the US Chamber of Commerce and some government and corporate leaders. But, in fact, the outsourced jobs in these companies were simply lost in the United States—Dr. Paul Craig Roberts points out in an article in *Global Research*:

> [over the last decade,] the net new jobs created in the U.S. have nothing to do with multinational corporations. These jobs consist of waitresses and bartenders, health care and social services (largely ambulatory health care), retail clerks, and while the bubble lasted, construction.[40]

Moreover, not only are older displaced workers unable to

find new jobs or sign up for disability, but even much younger workers have trouble finding jobs. As Roberts notes, 85 percent of recent college graduates plan to move back home with their parents because they couldn't earn enough to support themselves at the poor paying jobs available to them.

Additionally, the media and government statisticians underplay the real unemployment rate. The media sometimes claims the unemployment rate is less than 10 percent (9.6 percent as of this writing, according to Roberts), while the government claims it is 17 percent, but statistician John Williams says that the rate—based on unemployment claims—is 22 percent. So, it is hard to pin down the real number. Making the problem worse is that the media and government have praised the growth of private sector jobs, like claiming sixty-four thousand new jobs in a month. But this number ignores the loss of government jobs and the reality that "it takes about 150,000 new jobs each month to keep pace with labor force growth. In other words, a hundred thousand new jobs each month would be a fifty-thousand-jobs deficit."[41]

While the numbers are different, the same factors affect Baltimore and other major cities today. The number of jobs has been declining because of outsourcing and the decline of US manufacturing. Unfortunately, the blame is shifted to outside factors, like China manipulating the currency, which was originally triggered by "the greedy American poor who tried to live above their means," for instance, by taking out mortgages they could not afford. By making foreigners the scapegoats, the US government can avoid admitting its mistakes and avoid the responsibility for resolving the problem. Roberts puts the blame where it belongs: "An entire industry has grown up that points its finger at China and away from twenty years of corporate offshoring of US jobs and nine years of expensive and pointless US wars."[42]

One unfortunate result of this wrongheaded analysis is the erosion of the dollar, which has led to our trade deficit with China. That's because US corporations are offshoring their production made for the US markets to China and other countries to lower labor costs, so they can make more money. In turn, US workers suffer a decline of jobs, which contributes to the growing poverty of an underclass in Baltimore and many other cities in America.

Again, breaking the cycle starts with fixing the economy and with the government making adjustments to deal with the problems because of globalization. Training displaced workers can certainly help. But more needs to be done to keep jobs at home. One approach might be to provide tax credits to companies that hire US employees rather than sending the jobs overseas. Or maybe the new tech titans can be influenced to hire locally rather than globally. People here are eager to work, so why not devise a plan and figure this out?

Not Recognizing the Structural Forces Causing the Problem

One of the difficulties in fixing unemployment and poverty is the failure to recognize the underlying structural forces causing the problem or placing the blame in the wrong place.

A major structural force being ignored is the "increasing divergence in the attractiveness and performance between communities," according to Aaron M. Renn in a *Governing* article called "How Globalization Isolates Struggling Cities." As Renn points out using Indianapolis as an example, as certain suburbs improve, more residents and jobs are lured away from the city, so postindustrial communities and cities have fewer resources to rebuild with. An example of how this works is this: when a city seeks to attract businesses with various incentives, like tax breaks, but then the employees who receive middle-class wages of $18 an hour or more move to the nicest communities within forty miles, so those communities gain amenities because its residents have higher incomes. But many other communities are less advantaged, and the state government generally doesn't help, say by providing mass transit or new libraries and better schools.[43]

Another problem is that the struggling areas surrounding prosperous communities may not care to see already successful towns improve any further. Those communities with an influential block in the state legislature can stop further community improvements.

The result is a growing disconnect between a city that is doing well and poorer communities. There is a barrier in many states that contributes to a divergence between those who are better off in certain communities and poorer individuals elsewhere. The irony is that in response to globalization, cities and states are more interested in connecting with cities around the world—like to benefit from reduced costs for labor and manufacturing abroad—than in helping struggling areas back home.

But in order to solve the growing cycle of poverty in some sectors of the economy, it is necessary to reconnect these divergent areas and recognize that we are all in this together. As Renn writes:

> Removing this [structural barrier to change] requires a type of thinking and bridge-building that has fallen by the wayside in the contemporary economy, namely restoring connectivity between thriving cities and their broader but less well-off hinterlands.
>
> In the age of globalization, cities and states would rather build bridges to the world than to the town next door… This is the two-tier society we see developing nationally playing out at the local level. It creates a tug of war at the state-policy level, and it tears apart the whole notion that we are a commonwealth. It creates states that are "hives of warring interest."[44]

Thus, Renn urges building stronger links between neighboring towns and cities. He argues that larger metros and thriving regions should not only be given the "authority, tools, and financing they need to improve themselves and meet the demands of today's globalized, talent-based economy," but they should be expected to send tax remittances to the rest of the state and deploy some of their intellectual and policy resources to the problems facing the left-behind areas. As he puts it, "the losers need to let the winners get on with their winning, while the winners need to remember where they came from and who brought them to the dance."[45]

Likewise, when there is a divergence between impoverished neighborhoods of the city and wealthier ones, the city and state should pursue a similar policy of not only helping the winners, but contributing to the sections that are not doing so well. In this way, civic improvement is promoted at the state and city level. Otherwise, the poor will get poorer and the rich richer.

The Influence of Technological Change

Another big factor destroying jobs is the technology revolution, which contributes to poverty too. But even though outsourcing has contributed to the divergence between the haves and have-nots, many jobs would be lost regardless, because of improvements in technology. The result is that machines are replacing workers because they are faster, more productive, and less prone to errors. In other words, as machines have become better, there is less demand for human workers.

As Daniel W. Drezner points out in "Globalization and Baltimore," in the *Washington Post*, "the far bigger driver of these job losses is the creative destruction that comes from innovation and productivity increases."[46] The geographic shift in manufacturing employment to other countries is just a small factor in the decline of jobs. The big trend is toward more automation and productivity.

In fact, as Drezner notes, citing other research, the job reduction in the United States began well before China became a manufacturing power. Moreover, the number of workers in manufacturing has been falling almost everywhere, including China. The big driver is technology, reflected in the low or declining share of manufacturing jobs in virtually every major economy.

For example, the United Kingdom and Australia, according to the Organization for Economic Cooperation and Development, experienced a two-thirds drop in the number of manufacturing jobs since 1971. Though trade liberalization contributed to the loss of some manufacturing jobs, the major driver was technology.

A Combination of Influences

Certainly, there is a direct effect when a new technology brings automation and faster job performance, so less human labor is needed. Except to handle things the machines can't do—at least for now—like programming, adjusting the machines, and handling personalized customer service. However, the growth of new technologies has directly influenced other social and structural changes. For example, the new technologies have contributed to globalization, which has contributed to outsourcing jobs. And this decline in jobs has led to lower pay for those who want to work and no pay for those who can't find work. Then, that lower income has contributed to poverty in cities, which has in turn fueled the despair and anger that sparked the unrest in Baltimore.

All of these changes are related. For example, new technologies that automate jobs and push workers to the lower-wage service industry can lead to changes in the job market. Among these is a decline in manufacturing, because out-of-work employees don't have the skills to take on new jobs, as manufacturing companies automate to reduce costs. Then, since US workers lack the skills, this can lead to more outsourcing in countries that provide the needed workers.

These combined influences, in turn, mean that any solution to break the cycle has considered all of these and what is possible given the changes in society and the economy. For example, it may not be possible to halt the decline in manufacturing and the rise of other economies. But it might be possible to create a multifaceted solution.

One change introduced into the system might be providing assistance in adjusting to new jobs and also a training program to teach new skills required by the new technologies. Or training in other languages, to enable employees to better communicate with others around the world who are working with these technologies. Still another source of help might be assisting workers with transportation, so they can commute to jobs elsewhere.

Then, too, workers might need assistance with renting local housing, so they can stay nearer the job during the week, at a time when rents in cities like San Francisco are skyrocketing because of the influx of tech workers and money. Or perhaps workers could be assisted in obtaining the equipment they need to telecommute and work at home, like computers and video conferencing. In short, we must not only train workers with new skills, but make other social and economic changes to adapt society to the new socioeconomic order.

Fixing the Criminal Justice System to Break the Cycle

To a great extent, those who end up in the criminal justice system are there because of the overall social conditions that are influenced by the economics already described. This is because the low pay and few jobs has contributed to inner-city poverty, which are predominantly made up of African Americans. Some who live in areas of high poverty have shown a tendency to involve themselves in gang activity and the underground drug industry, which contribute to the high crime rates and the spread of drug abuse, all of which leads to more citizen-police encounters. These encounters result in the high incarceration rate and the high incidence of police violence against blacks, especially young black males. Moreover, not only is the arrest rate higher among African Americans, but those arrested are more likely to be convicted and receive harsher sentences.

Thus, there is a cycle that can be traced back to social and economic changes, resulting in job losses and reduced incomes, and then to more crime, arrests, and incarceration. Accordingly, anything that might disrupt this cycle at any point could reduce the arrest and incarceration rates, although some social policies might be directed to reducing arrest and incarceration rates directly.

One symptom of this problem is the high number of misconduct lawsuits against police officers, usually arising from encounters with young black males. As Mark Puente describes in "Sun Investigates: Some Baltimore Police Officers Face Repeated Misconduct Lawsuits,"[47] a number of Baltimore police officers have faced multiple lawsuits. But in general, police leaders, city attorneys, and other top officials have not acknowledged the high number of officers repeatedly facing police brutality lawsuits. These numbers are huge. In Baltimore alone, since 2011, police officers have been hit with 317 lawsuits for civil rights and constitutional violations, like false imprisonment, assault, and false arrest. The result has been $5.7 million in settlements and court judgments, and in every case, the people who received settlements or won court judgments were cleared of any criminal charges, suggesting the original arrest was fraudulent.

Another problem in the cycle of injustice in the criminal justice system is that some of the officers charged with repeat misconduct lawsuits have moved into other districts or positions, in part because of civil service rules and in part because of officers not reporting the use of force, though the reporting is required. So, the city, police, and public are not aware of this behavior, and the pattern continues. This brutality and misconduct often occur when an officer is arresting a suspect and then adds false charges to protect the officer involved. As Puente notes:

> Some city practices, including the sparse information provided to the public about proposed settlements, have limited the public's knowledge about police misconduct. In such settlement agreements, the city and its police officers do not acknowledge any wrongdoing, and the residents who sued are prohibited from talking in public or to the news media about the allegations.

This pattern of nonreporting means that officers who repeatedly engage in misconduct are protected, while the beating—even though the victim is compensated and the charges are dismissed—can have lasting consequences for the victim. For example, a beating can lead to permanent injury, making it difficult for the individual to work again. Any charges, even if later dismissed, might damage the individual's ability to get certain jobs, like in the security field—even if the arrest is expunged, the record of it might remain in that person's personnel file.

Another big problem is the high incarceration rate of lower-income individuals, primarily young black youths in the inner cities, who end up in prison for nonviolent offenses, like drug possession. The police are more likely to arrest these lower-income individuals for these offenses, often after stopping them for questioning or for minor infractions, like littering. A common scenario is that a stop for questioning can lead to the discovery of drugs in a pat-down or a flight to avoid arrest. So, not only are these low-income individuals more likely to be arrested in the first place, they are more likely to be sent to prison and receive longer sentences than other offenders. The prisons are filled to capacity with nonviolent offenders, which contributes to poverty in their families, since the offender cannot contribute to the family.

In these situations, the fix lies in the criminal justice system itself. One fix is a more transparent system, so that the police leadership, city officials, and the public know about these incidents. Moreover, police supervisors must mandate that officers report such incidents. The use of body and dashboard cameras will help to make these incidents more transparent too.

Another solution would be to train officers to be more careful when they approach suspects or make an arrest to avoid unnecessary brutality. Often these incidents occur because an officer becomes angry when a suspect resists arrest or is verbally disrespectful, so the officer responds with unnecessary force. So more training is needed to help police officers deal with difficult situations and better manage anger. Then, too, the training might involve using less violent methods to control suspects, like a Taser instead of a baton or gun to subdue them, where possible. Additionally, officers need more training in stepping back after a suspect has been subdued, rather than continuing to hit him.

Still another fix is reducing the number of prisoners incarcerated for nonviolent offenses, including drug possession and low-level sales. To some extent, a response to this problem has already occurred through President Obama using his clemency power to commute the sentences of nonviolent drug offenders. However, as described by Peter Baker in a July 2015 *New York Times* article: "Obama Plans Broader Use of Clemency to Free Nonviolent Drug Offenders,"[48] Obama's efforts do not go far enough and the reviews of petitions for clemency are stuck in a bureaucratic traffic jam. As Baker notes, Obama is expected to commute over eighty sentences, but that is only a handful of the thousands of inmates who have applied. And only a small fraction of these petitions have even reached the president's desk for a signature. Also, the US Sentencing Commission has retroactively reduced the sentences for over 9,500 inmates with drug offenses, nearly three-quarters of them black or Hispanic from the inner cities, which has contributed to earlier release. And there is hope for the future in that legislators from both parties have come together to overhaul the criminal justice system, including reducing excessive sentencing.

But those changes should occur quickly, not stall in bureaucracy and negotiations. We must move quickly to release even more of these low-level offenders. One problem is that clemency or reduced sentence does not expunge it from the person's record or restore the civil rights taken away by that conviction. But the president does have the power to give a pardon, which is "an act of presidential forgiveness" that "wipes away any remaining legal liabilities from a conviction." So, we need for more pardons, not just commutations and sentence reductions by the US Sentencing Commission.

And we must speed up the process. One group that has helped prepare clemency petitions for inmates is the Clemency Project, which since 2013 has gotten assistance from over fifteen hundred lawyers, more than fifty law firms, and more than twenty law schools. But as Baker describes, the process takes a long time, since the lawyers have to search for the documentation needed. As of July 2015, they sent out only about fifty applications to the Justice Department—a drop in the bucket of the Justice Department's over 6,600 applications. Since 2014 I have been a part of a Clemency Project workgroup. As part of the workgroup we have suggested many procedures to support prisoners after they are released.

In short, we must speed up the release of these men and women and get them back to their families. And the process must include expunging the records of many of these returning citizens so they do not have to put these convictions on job applications, making it much easier for them to find work, helping to break the cycle of poverty.

Improving the Educational System

Another way to break the cycle is to improve the educational system, since studies have repeatedly shown that increasing education increases job opportunities and pay. But in Baltimore and other cities, the education for children in the inner cities is much worse than elsewhere.

As Emily Badger points out in a *Washington Post* article, "How Baltimore and Cities Like It Hold Back Poor Black Children as They Grow Up," geography plays a huge role in shaping a child's chances of future success. After researchers collected a list of the hundred largest counties in America, they found that Baltimore was at the bottom as far as the odds of advancing and breaking out of the cycle of poverty. This is especially true for boys, with devastating effects on their future. As Raj Chetty and Nathaniel Hendren found, every year that a poor boy spends growing up in an economically disadvantaged place reduces his potential earnings as an adult. For example, in Baltimore, a poor boy's earnings as an adult fall by 1.5 percent for every year he lives there, with the result that when he is twenty-six, he will earn 28 percent less than if he grew up in an average city in America.[49]

A key reason poor children fare so poorly is that they have to "contend with struggling schools and less social capital, because racial and economic segregation further isolates them away from good schools and better neighborhoods." Yet, if those same children and their families moved to better neighborhoods, they did better. As Chetty, Hendren, and Katz found in revisiting the children of a "Moving to Opportunity" the government experiment that started in the mid-1990s, when HUD offered poor families housing vouchers to move to better neighborhoods. Those children earned about 30 percent more than children who didn't move. In fact, the taxes that they paid was enough to offset the cost of the program. They had higher college attendance rates, lived in better neighborhoods, and were less likely to be single parents—a good example of breaking the cycle of poverty. As Jonah Goldberg notes in a *Townhall* article, the key to breaking the cycle of poverty was getting the kids out of poor neighborhoods, because "the earlier kids got out of impoverished neighborhoods, the better they did over their lifetimes." They were "more likely to go to college and earn more." The researchers further found that giving kids with an average age of eight a voucher to move out of a low-poverty area increased their lifetime earnings by $302,000, and girls were 26 percent less likely to become single mothers.[50]

Later, when Chetty and his colleagues looked at the earnings of five million families around the United States for over seventeen years, they found that neighborhoods matter. It is hard to pull out any one factor, though social scientists have argued that certain factors play a more critical role. Some feel a child's peers are most important. Others claim that parents, especially those who are married, play a central role. Still others point to schools, criminal justice policies, and racial attitudes as key factors. But the problem with trying to figure out how much weight to give different factors is that all of these factors interact with and influence each other, and in very poor neighborhoods they combine to make problems even worse.

So, the neighborhood where a child grows up is vital because culture matters, and culture includes everything from social norms to legal structures, putting poor kids at a disadvantage when they grow up. For instance, Chetty notes that "every extra year of childhood in Baltimore's worst areas reduces earnings by 1.39 percent for low-income boys."[51] It is a pattern echoed in other low-income areas, though the specific numbers may differ from city to city.

Thus, as this study shows, one way to break the cycle is for families in high-poverty neighborhoods to move to a better environment, where the crime rate is down, and schools and other social indicators are better. However, the vast majorities of families cannot move.

In other words, since it is not possible for every child or family to move, we need more neighborhood-wide programs to break the cycle—not just for individual children, but for the whole community. To that end, programs must be created to involve residents in raising themselves out of poverty. The government might provide some funding and some neighborhood outreach coordinators to light the spark, but then the residents have to demand this change, they need to understand the benefits for themselves, their families, and their community. Community institutions like churches, need to be mobilized, too. As they say, it takes a village, or in this case, it takes a whole neighborhood, people working together to pull themselves and one another out of poverty. People must see the value of making this effort, and then they need help in putting these ideas into practice, so neighborhoods can break the poverty cycle, one neighborhood at a time.

CHAPTER 8
ZERO TOLERANCE

After spending almost twelve years in prison for dealing heroin and cocaine in Baltimore, I unfortunately know more about incarceration than I ever wanted to know. My journey from where I was then, a guy in the streets, to where I am now in life has been a dramatic shift. The upside to this experience is that as an advocate, I can have a powerful effect on issues like criminal justice reform, as I understand both sides of the matter. The sound of the steel cell door closing behind me as I walked into this dark place called the penitentiary stays with me even today. I would be remiss if I didn't make a real commitment to make a difference in the lives of others.

With the incarceration rate in Baltimore and American among the highest in the world, how do we make sure that returning citizens or the formerly incarcerated become part of the solution instead of part of the problem? At one time, Mayor O'Malley spearheaded a zero-tolerance policy in which the police were encouraged to make arrests for even the most minor crimes in the inner cities. The thinking was that this crackdown on everyday crimes would discourage more serious crimes.

But did this zero-tolerance policy reduce crime or just increase our prison populations? If we as a society are going to place individuals in prison and jail, we have to be absolutely certain that the policies we have in place are just and fair.

Mayor O'Malley's Zero-Tolerance Policy

I began thinking about how Mayor O'Malley's zero-tolerance policy might have unwittingly contributed to the demonstrations and riots after the Freddie Gray incident because this policy created an environment of mistrust between the police and community. I thought about the problems of policing in urban areas generally and about the positive results that could come from alternative approaches to reintegrating the formerly incarcerated into the community. For instance, workforce development programs, fair sentencing laws, and community policing.

Zero tolerance—which is sometimes called "broken windows policing"—involves cracking down on minor offenses on the theory that this will reduce major crime too. According to this approach, the police should be more aggressive in policing inner-city minority criminals, because that's where the criminals are. However, this approach also means that if the police focus on patrolling certain areas and assume that every young man they see might be a potential or likely criminal, they will engage in more searches and more arrests. The result will be that a higher percentage of young men in the neighborhood will have police records. Then this higher statistic justifies continuing aggressive police tactics, as Eugene Robinson points out in a *Washington*

Post article "It's Time to Seriously Rethink 'Zero-Tolerance' Policing."[52]

This type of policing assumes that it will deter criminals through a greater awareness of the police presence in the area. Another expected deterrent is strict punishments, which makes it clear that criminals will receive serious penalties for crime. But in fact, the main targets of this type of policing—minor offenders, gang members, and the poor—commit many of these everyday crimes because of the necessity of poverty and substance abuse. Such crimes can only be reduced by changing the structure of society, not by threats of punishment.

Also, in theory, a zero-tolerance policy establishes firm guidelines on what types of arrests officers can make for different types of crimes. But in practice, it gives the police almost unlimited power in low-income communities, and they are able to stop, search, and harass individuals whenever they please. And typically they target certain groups, usually African Americans and other ethnic minorities—so we are arrested and labeled as criminals more frequently than whites, Asians, and other groups.[53]

The irony is that O'Malley's zero-tolerance policy had the immediate effect of reducing crime and making Baltimore a safer city, and he gained widespread support for this policy. Its early success even contributed to his campaign to run for president.

But in the long term, the policy may have contributed to the eruption in Baltimore because it created a large population of formerly incarcerated people who had trouble finding jobs and reintegrating into society. It also contributed to a growing distrust of the police in the African-American community because the police were so proactive in making arrests for just about anything. Even minor offenses, like dropping a candy wrapper on the street, could result in an arrest and leave the arrestee with a record, making it difficult to get a job, even if the arrest didn't result in a conviction or imprisonment.

But I'm getting ahead of myself. Let me describe the zero-tolerance policy in more detail and the recent comments about it in the wake of O'Malley's aborted run for the presidency. Then, I'll consider these other issues dealing with integrating returning citizens and the formerly incarcerated into the community, not only in Baltimore but across the nation

The Crackdown on Crime Under O'Malley

O'Malley served as Baltimore's mayor from 1999 to 2007 and went on to become the governor of Maryland. In his brief run, O'Malley played up his achievement in promoting the police crackdown that led to a reduction in drug violence and homicides. That reduction is certainly true. When he first became mayor in 1999, Baltimore was a very violent city, in part because of the widespread poverty that primarily affected the African-American community. At the time, the police relations with our community were already strained, much as they were in inner cities throughout the nation, where the police were often seen as the enemy, rather than a partner of the community.

But soon after O'Malley became mayor, as described by Paul Schwartzman and John Wagner in the *Washington Post*,[54] the crackdown began with a new police strategy of making arrests for even minor offenses, like loitering and littering. Some individuals were arrested multiple times. The effectiveness of the strategy at first—for instance, homicides dropped 16 percent, was a major contributing factor in him winning 67 percent of the state Democratic primary vote in 2003. O'Malley even supported the creation of a civilian review board, which is a good thing, and the number of police shootings declined, another good thing.

However, the downside of the police crackdown was creating community-police distrust, and the drop in crime might have been achieved in ways that could have built trust, improved local economic conditions, and integrated returning citizens and the formerly incarcerated into the community. Let me explain.

The big problem with the police crackdown is that the number of arrests in Baltimore zoomed through the stratosphere. By 2005, there were 108,448 individuals arrested in the city—about one-sixth of the city's population of 600,000 people—and a very large percentage of the arrestees ended up in jail. The result was not only high costs for this mass incarceration, but enduring social costs, because all these individuals now had arrest records, making it difficult for them to find jobs. This many arrests contributed to destabilizing the family and community, in that many arrestees had trouble supporting—and therefore staying with—their families, and that contributed to higher costs for social welfare and health benefits. In other words, on the surface, the high arrest and mass-incarceration strategy might appear to have solved the problem. But it resulted in other social problems that aren't factored into those claims of its success.

Then there is the issue of trust between police and the community, which affected not only those arrested, but their family members and friends, as they too became victims of their loved one's incarceration. The separation made staying in touch difficult and the family income was decimated because loved one's had difficulties getting a job and making a decent income when released.

So, as much as former Mayor O'Malley may tout his great success in reducing crime in Baltimore, this crime reduction had a social cost—to the individual arrested, his family, and the community. This policy contributed to the resentment and mistrust of the police, so when the Freddie Gray incident occurred after he was arrested for a minor offense and subsequently died in the back of the police van, the conditions were ripe for the community to erupt in anger.

Attitudes Today about the Zero-Tolerance Policy

Again, many people think O'Malley's approach to crime was a key factor leading to the protests and riots in response to Freddie Gray's death. To get a sense of these attitudes, I followed a Daily Kos discussion online. Daily Kos is a blog with political analysis on US current events in which the people of Baltimore talked about Martin O'Malley on April 28, 2015. In general, the people viewed his actions as mayor as contributing to a police state in Baltimore, which bred the distrust that boiled over after Gray died, although O'Malley began to distance himself from the problems resulting from his policy. Here is a sampling of these comments, indicating the belief of many that his actions contributed to the sad state of affairs in Baltimore today.[55]

User Floridageorge wrote:

> O'Malley was the architect for the type of policing that we have seen here in Baltimore…A high rate of stop-and-frisk…so it really created an environment where you had 127 murders or police-killings between 1992 and 2012, a lot of that is in the period in which he is in office and… in which he is governor. So, a lot of this has taken place under his watch and only now today are people really finding out about it, but it was going on the whole time. The former governor has a large, large responsibility to bear in terms of explaining the kind of police state we have here in Baltimore. From prominent NAACP leaders in Baltimore regarding his role in this, a role they claim "sowed distrust." He talks as if he were just an innocent bystander, when in fact he was/is directly involved… Baltimore civic leaders are accusing him of being the catalyst, the "root," of the current problem. Since that is the case, you really don't think he should address those comments?…Sure, the issue is being dealt with by others, but the root cause as to the WHY in that particular community involves him, and to a lot of folks in that community, it all started with him introducing what they feel were unconstitutional and racist policies.

Another user with the handle Le Champignon responded:

> Your boring former governor doesn't get above 6 percent in any of these polls, and in fact is at 1 percent in

several. There is no appetite for O'Malley, unlike Obama at a similar stage of the campaign. That isn't going to change, particularly now that Baltimore burns from policies that he started during his tenure as mayor.

Floridageorge responded:

Baltimore, zero-tolerance. In the tradition of Giuliani, it relied heavily on arresting people (primarily members of the AA community) for nothing, absolutely nothing. Just standing around would lead to an arrest. That is how he arrested 100,000 people out of 600,000 residents in JUST ONE YEAR...That is FACT, not disputed by anyone, not even the fiercest O'Malley supporters. One hundred thousand people out of 600,000 residents means that every sixth person who resides in Baltimore was arrested that year. And...if you take out babies, toddlers, children, very old people, you probably have it that every SECOND (or at least every THIRD) "eligible" resident of the city of Baltimore was arrested that year. I highly doubt you can find any other city in the United States with such incredibly high arrest rates in any given year (relative to the city's population,) even Giuliani's New York. Yes, he [O'Malley] got crime under control. But at what cost? Arresting basically every black male in sight is something to be proud of because it curbs crime?

While a few of O'Malley's supporters pointed to his record of reducing crime, creating a citizen's police review board, twice winning an election, getting 67 percent of the Democratic primary vote on his way to a second term, and leaving Baltimore in a stronger position as a city, the overall opinion faulted him for his draconian police policies and link these to what happened to the city after Freddie Gray's death. It's a point of view I strongly support, since zero-tolerance policing unfairly targets the poor and minority communities, resulting in more arrests for minor offenses, some of which might not even be crimes. Then this high level of arrests contributes to a climate of citizen-police distrust and conflict, resulting in even more arrests for minor crimes and a growing anger throughout the community that can lead to protests and demonstrations when an inflammatory incident occurs.

Policing in Urban Areas

The issue of zero-tolerance policing also raises the question of the role of policing in urban areas, especially in low-income and minority communities. These policies need to be reviewed and assessed, too, because they can contribute to community-police conflict and mistrust as well. The development of an urban policing strategy goes back to the 1970s, when many urbanites moved to the suburbs because of congestion and crime rates in the inner cities. This phenomenon, called "white flight," saw the migration of whites to the suburbs, which contributed to growing poverty in the inner cities along with an eroding tax base. This poverty, in turn, spurred an increase in crime in the inner city, where the remaining residents were mainly members of lower-income minority groups. Poverty also contributed to a fragmentation of the community, a rending of family bonds, and an increase in drug and alcohol addiction and mental illness. Meanwhile, those outside this community, especially in the suburbs, tended to see those in the inner cities as a kind of "throw-away society" or "skid row," where the goal was to contain the crime and arrest and convict the criminals.[56]

That attitude has, in turn, led to the development of special handling techniques by the police in the inner city, focused on "containing" the area through various means, including narcotics enforcement, getting the homeless off the streets, cracking down on gun violence, and making arrests for minor offenses and uncivil actions that are part of the zero-tolerance strategy.

Some cities have also used micro-policing to target selected hot spots, where violence is concentrated among certain groups of people, like youths aged fifteen to twenty-four, who are sometimes in gangs. For example, in Boston, 1 percent of the youth in this age group were responsible for half of all the murders and 70 percent of the shootings, and most were involved in gangs. So now some cities are using a more localized approach to policing, along with computerized gang audits to provide officers with the latest gang intelligence so they can target the specific streets and individuals responsible for the vast majority of urban violence.

The result of this micro-policing has proved to be effective in many areas, according to research from the Institution for Social and Policy Studies at Yale University. For example, the Project Safe Neighborhoods (PSN) in Chicago resulted in a 37 percent homicide rate decrease and Ceasefire-Boston resulted in a 68 percent reduction in gang violence.[57]

In my view, this kind of targeting to crack down on violent crime makes more sense than the zero-tolerance policy of making arrests for minor offenses. This targeting also helps to make the community safer, which is what the vast majority of the community wants. Plus, I think the police in urban communities need to keep in mind the code of conduct for law enforcement officials, which has been developed by the international community for policing urban spaces around the world. Among the most important of these policies are these:[58]

- Respect and protect human dignity, and maintain and uphold the human
- rights of all persons.
- Law enforcement officials may use force only when strictly necessary and to
- the extent required for the performance of their duty;
- Protect the health of persons in custody.

At the same time, some of the United Nations guidelines on how the police should play a more proactive role to integrate with the community and prevent crime are especially helpful. These guidelines are:

- Provide a visible presence.
- Become more integrated in the community.
- Help to mediate and resolve conflicts.
- Offer support to victims.
- Act as mentors and role models.
- Participate in local crime prevention partnerships.

In short, in place of a zero-tolerance program, I think we need a strategy that embraces getting tough on the perpetrators of violent crimes, along with outreach to integrate with community members. Based on input from community members, some ways to do this are to help to resolve conflicts and to participate in crime prevention initiatives.

Workforce Development Programs for Ex-Offenders and the Formerly Incarcerated

Some could possibly say that my friend Twin from West Baltimore is a habitual criminal and, therefore, doesn't deserve another chance. He's been in and out of prison almost his entire life, starting at age sixteen. But who are we to say how many chances are too many chances? We have to get out of the business of throwing people away like they don't matter. Every human desires as many chances as possible to get it right, because once they finally do turn the corner, the sky really can be the limit. It took me several chances before I got it right and here I am.

One strategy that has helped reduce violent crime, drug addiction, and gang activity is helping returning citizens and the formerly incarcerated find jobs. Just as education is the key to better jobs and better jobs make individuals more productive members of society, workforce development programs have a similar effect on the success of men and women returning from incarceration. For them, workforce development programs provide the training and guidance they need to obtain jobs.

Such a strategy is crucial now because of the number of individuals in prison and the costs of maintaining the correction system. As of 2014, about one in four US working-age adults has a criminal record, which serves as a significant barrier to acquiring a quality job.[59] As of 2008, there were 6.1 million formerly incarcerated individuals in the United States, and in 2012, over 1.5 million men and women were incarcerated in state and federal prisons, according to Jacob Wascalus in "Development Programs to Help Ex-Offenders Join the Workforce." In turn, the cost of corrections is huge. In 2010, the federal, state, and local governments spent over $80 billion on corrections.[60]

Thus, programs to reduce recidivism not only help the individual, but society as a whole, by reducing the cost of crimes and recidivism. The research shows these programs reduce recidivism by helping former inmates find and keep jobs.

Let me give some examples of how well these programs work. Typically, they involve training returning citizens in performing different kinds of jobs and giving them the skills to apply for jobs successfully. Then, during a follow-up period, program staffers check on how well they are doing. At the same time, prospective employers must be encouraged to give formerly incarcerated individuals a second chance. Because many hold back from employing these individuals because of fear of theft or embezzlement. But generally, this fear of becoming a victim is a myth, since most returning citizens turn out to be loyal, hardworking employees, grateful for the chance to get a good job again.

That's what these programs do. They help give men and women a second chance to reintegrate into society, which results in reduced crime and incarceration rates.

Such programs are spreading around the United States. For example, in California, Ban the Box legislation was passed in the summer of 2014 to improve the employment opportunities of nearly seven million state residents, while similar bills were passed in New Jersey, Illinois, Washington, DC, and many other cities and states, according to Juan Sebastian Arias in "Enhancing the Employment Chances for Formerly Incarcerated Americans."[61] Another example is the Georgia Justice Project's "Enhance the Chance" program, using positive language to appeal to a more conservative citizenry.

There have also been efforts around the country to persuade the public, policymakers, and employers to support "ban the box" or "enhance the chance" efforts, like the Job Opportunities Task Force, which was created in Maryland to advocate for legislation to help returning citizens find jobs. As part of this effort, the Task Force has sought testimony from former inmates describing their difficulties in finding employment because of their criminal record, although they are otherwise qualified.[62] Such efforts are truly needed to help members of the public, government, and prospective employers realize the barriers to employment faced by former inmates who want to work in order to gain support for their efforts to get a second chance.

Another state in the forefront of this programming is Minnesota. These programs are crucial, because as Jacob Wascalus notes about Minnesota: "For an ex-offender reentering mainstream society, finding legitimate, gainful employment is an essential step toward creating a productive new life. But... getting hired can be a formidable challenge for someone with a criminal record."[63]

That's why a number of organizations in Minnesota have developed various programs to help returning citizens find and keep good living-wage jobs. These programs help them obtain the basic requirements for work, which include developing soft skills (like how to work with people), a basic education, and skills in the industry they are seeking to enter.

One of these Minnesota programs is AccessAbility's Project Connect program,[64] which offers career training through a three-step program whereby returning citizens take on more and more responsibility and independence. At first, all of the participants are unemployed, and from the first day, they earn wages. Initially, they work at one of AccessAbility's business services, where they work at unskilled jobs like recycling materials or helping with packaging and assembly. In the second phase, they work for one of the businesses owned by AccessAbilty, but at an offsite employer, and typically they do light industrial work. In the third and final phase, they get a permanent job with the phase-two employer or an outside business. The program lasts for three months to a year, depending on the participant. The results speak for themselves. Over 250 formerly incarcerated individuals graduated from the program and got jobs and, after a year, 91 percent of them were still on the job.

Another Minnesota program is run by Twin Cities RISE,[65] which focuses on personal empowerment. RISE uses what it calls a "long-term, high-touch model" that not only teaches the soft and hard skills, but helps the returning citizens examine and alter some of their personal behaviors and attitudes that have stood in the way of getting good, legitimate jobs. For instance, they learn to regulate their emotions, feel empathy, and develop self-esteem.[66] Generally, those ex-offenders who finish the program obtain a job that pays at least $20,000 a year—and on average they earn $25,000 a year, much more than the average $6,100 a year they earned before participating in the program. As in the AccessAbility's Project Connect, the formerly incarcerated individuals tend to keep their jobs too. About 81 percent stayed in their job for at least a year, and 70 percent remained for a second year.

To give one more example from Minnesota, SOAR Career Solutions [67] has been helping formerly incarcerated individuals reintegrate into the community through its Community Offender Reentry Program. Like these other two programs, SOAR assigned a development coach or case manager to each participant. But the program doesn't wait until the returning citizens are back in the community. Instead, it starts working with them two to three months before they are released from prison to ease the transition from prison into society. Then, once they are out of prison, they participate in pre-employment and training programs to learn the hard and soft skills as in the other programs. Plus, offenders can take training courses offered through grants from Minnesota's Department of Employment and Economic Development and local foundations. A big advantage is that many courses offer opportunities to get certificates that are recognized in their industry, like in welding, machine operation, and truck driving. Additionally, SOAR connects ex-offenders to services to help them reenter society, like housing, transportation, and help with mental health issues.[68]

In short, these are just some of the programs developed in states around the United States to help returning citizens and the formerly incarcerated acquire the hard and soft skills needed to successfully find and keep jobs.

In turn, government support can fund these programs. For example, pay-for-success Initiatives—also known as social impact bonds—provide public funds to encourage innovation and reward initiatives that show successful results. Two such programs are New York State's Pay for Success Initiative and Massachusetts' Juvenile Justice Pay for Success Initiative.[69] A similar model could be used to help funding Workforce Development Programs for ex-offenders and the formerly incarcerated.

Fair Sentencing Laws

The Fair Sentencing Laws passed by the US Congress have also reduced the length of sentence for certain types of nonviolent crimes. The first of these Fair Sentencing Laws was the Fair Sentencing Act (FSA), passed in 2010, which reduced the disparity in the sentences for offenses involving crack cocaine as opposed to powder cocaine from 100:1 to 18:1, according to a discussion of the act by the ACLU.[70] This disparity was patently unfair because crack and powder are just different forms of the same drug.

As pointed out in the ACLU discussion, this disparity was especially disturbing because most people arrested for crack offenses were African American, so, "On average, under the 100:1 regime, African Americans served virtually as much time in prison for nonviolent drug offenses as whites did for violent offenses." Adjusting this disparity helped those affected by these laws gain confidence in the criminal justice system.

Then, in 2011, the US Sentencing Commission decided to apply these new guidelines retroactively to individuals who were sentenced before the law passed. As a result, over twelve thousand people—85 percent of them African-Americans—had their sentences reviewed by a federal judge and possibly reduced, though they are still subject to the original mandatory minimums passed before the 2010 FSA law.

Even some states have acted to reduce sentence disparities, like California, which passed the California Fair Sentencing Act to eliminate the disparity in sentencing, probation, and asset forfeiture for possessing crack cocaine versus powder cocaine for sale, which became effective in January 2015.[71]

Then, on February 12, 2015, Congress introduced the Smarter Sentencing Act of 2015, which makes the Fair Sentencing Act of 2010 retroactive, so 8,800 people currently serving sentences for possessing crack contain can now petition the court to review their case. A goal of this act is to reduce the over-criminalization of offenses by requiring federal agencies to reveal to the public a list of all federal crimes and their penalties. This helps to create a more just criminal justice system—to put the "just" back into "justice" so to speak.[72]

Additionally, the bill cuts the mandatory minimum sentence in half for individuals who are only involved in transporting or storing drugs or money. The bill has gained broad support by both Democrats and Republicans because of the need for sentencing reform. As Della Anderson points out in an article for the Friends Committee on National Legislation, "In the past 30 years the federal prison population has increased more than 500 percent and more than half of those are in prison for nonviolent drug offenses. The cost of this mass-use of incarceration to the American tax-payer: $6.8 billion annually."[73]

A benefit of these changes is that they will help nonviolent ex-offenders return more quickly to the community, just as the workforce development programs will reintegrate them. Meanwhile, the long history of unfair sentencing and the difficulty ex-offenders have finding jobs in the past has contributed to Baltimore's festering anger that erupted in protests and demonstrations.

Community Policing

Community policing is one of the most promising responses to overcome the sense of community-police distrust. Done right, this becomes a partnership between the police and community. The approach has been around for about two decades, in the form of crime-prevention programs, and civilian community-policing coordinators to assess community needs and liaise between the community and the police.

One such program was in Oakland, California in the late 1990s, which divided the city into a dozen areas. A community-policing coordinator was assigned to each one, and one of their tasks was to set up local crime prevention meetings that were held in a host's home and led by a police officer. The city also conducted a Citizens Police Academy, in which citizens participated in classes led by officers for fourteen weeks to explain police operations. Thereafter, program graduates could join a Citizen Police Academy Alumni Association to help support the police, like putting on local officer-appreciation events. This worked well for a time, until a budget crunch dismantled the program.[74]

Generally, these programs are designed to empower officers to identify and solve community problems proactively. The approach involves three key components: developing community partnerships, participating in problem-solving with community members, and implementing activities in line with community wants and needs. To this end, the police partner with government agencies, including probation and parole, health and human services, schools, and other law enforcement agencies. The underlying theory is that by creating interactive partnerships between law enforcement and members of the community, the police can better resolve public safety problems and combat crime, particularly the crimes considered most in need of attention by community members.[75]

According to the Bureau of Justice Assistance, community policing is considered one of a number of community-based crime prevention programs in which community residents actively work with local government agencies to look at issues which contribute to crime, delinquency, and disorder, and play key roles in identifying problems and planning for solutions. This includes things like the neighborhood watch, in which citizen groups organize to prevent and report neighborhood crime and disorder, commonly by holding meetings to discuss issues with a police officer. Often such programs involve forming police-community partnerships to address crime-related problems.[76]

There is even an Office of Community Oriented Policing Services (COPS) in the US Department of Justice that is dedicated to promoting trust and mutual respect between police and the communities they serve. As the COPS website puts it:

> This concept is the foundation of community policing and ensures that police and community stakeholders partner in solving our nation's crime challenges. Community policing is a law enforcement philosophy that focuses on community partnerships, problem-solving and organizational transformation. The COPS Office mission is to advance public safety through community policing.[77]

The theory is that "when police and communities work together, they more effectively address underlining issues, change negative patterns, and focus resources." To this end, the COPS Office plays a key role in enacting the attorney general's Smart on Crime Initiative by focusing on "fairer enforcement, crime prevention, and the improvement of relationships with minority populations."[78]

While this approach sounds great in theory, often these policies don't make their way down to the local community, or at least community members and leaders aren't aware of these partnerships in their own community. So, distrust between police and community members simmers and later erupts when something like the Freddie Gray issue happens.

Thus, it would seem a police-community partnership is needed to overcome this divide between police and community members—but it needs to be more of a grassroots community-led effort, not one developed by criminal justice bureaucrats. Even though they may have great theories, there is a disconnect when putting it into practice. We need a police-citizen partnership. But the way it is implemented needs to be reconsidered so that citizens feel more involved and take the lead.

• • • • • •

The calm after the storm in Baltimore had a welcoming effect on many of us. It was a time to breathe and reflect on the historic nature of what had just happened. Now it was time to look ahead as much as we could. What was next for Charm City, the place we all called home? How could we use this moment to work toward the betterment of Baltimore and its citizens?

Once things really began to settle down across the city I had a chance to sit and talk with one of Baltimore's rising young stars, Dayvon Love. Dayvon is the director of public policy for Leaders of a Beautiful Struggle. His group is doing some great work in the city with young people.

Kevin Shird: Dayvon, tell me a little more about your organization.

Dayvon Love: We're an organization that was founded in 2010, many of us former high school and college policy debaters. Policy debate is one of the most rigorous academic activities that exists, and policy debate is a feeder for many major public policy institutions—think tanks and the like. Our organization is a grassroots political advocacy organization, a think tank. We train our people on public policy using the tool of policy debate, and we do advocacy in the public policy arena, one issue that's pertinent to black people.

Kevin Shird: What made you want to get into this kind of work?

Dayvon Love: The training that I got in policy debate. One of the things that I realized—because again, it's a very elite, white activity—and when I was competing in it, I realized that there were institutions where folks got a chance to go and be a part of the institutions that would craft the policy agenda. Our form of debate, our style of debate, was unique, because we put forward academic and intellectual innovations. They're about challenging institutional racism and white supremacy in public policy spaces. It gave us a unique perspective, and we felt the unique contribution we could make to Baltimore was having a think tank that could address the issues that face the most marginalized folks in our communities, particularly people of African descent, given that many of the interest groups that represent some of the issues that affect our communities often times are not of or from the communities that face those issues.

You go to Annapolis, for instance, or city hall, a lot of the lobbyists that lobby on our behalf are often folks that are not of or from our communities. So, we felt like it was important to form an organization that does public policy advocacy from a perspective that is rooted in black radical tradition and the idea of building powerful communities to determine their own destiny.

Kevin Shird: You say the last few months. Now, Baltimore has gone through a lot of transitions in different perspectives. Where do we go from here? How do we fix what has been broken for decades? Give me your view on that whole situation. Maybe we could start with the history.

Dayvon Love: It's really important that we look at many of these issues from the perspective that our society is structured on the principal of racism and white supremacy. I think a lot of times when people talk about racism, they think about it as a character flaw. They think about it in terms of talking about an individual. But when we talk about racism, we're talking about the system, the configuration of institutions in civic society that organize themselves in such a way where it benefits white folks, the collective, economic, political, social interests of white people.

At the core of this, it means that black folks don't have the collective institutional wherewithal to be able to protect and advance their own interests. When you look at enslavement. A lot of times we look at enslavement...as, like, a moral issue, but one of the things we challenge people to do is [to] look at it from a political, economic, issue perspective. You can see the wealth acquisition activity that white folks are able to collectively participate in created pockets of wealth and that simultaneously undermined black folks from participating in this wealth acquisition activity. This is the anchor, the basis of the ability to build institutions that could advance one's quality of life.

We fast forward all the way to the past few months, what we see is communities that are capital deprived, that don't have the kind of functional institutions necessary to address the problems that really culminated in the April riots. A lot of those issues with things that were bubbling under the surface, but they culminated in April.

If you don't have the institutional capacity to address those issues, then that's why we have the uprising. I think, just in terms of how we got to where we got to, it's important to understand if there isn't an investment made in a community's ability to fix its own problems, then you're going to have to immediately start depending on government, depending on philanthropy.

They don't have the ability to produce for themselves a world that is their own. When people don't have ownership of the institutions that govern their lives, then people aren't necessarily invested in it. I think that's really what a genesis of the problem is in terms of a solution.

It's important to have the proper framework. I think a lot of people's framework for the solution is predicated on notions of black inferiority, right? The idea that black folks in Baltimore are broken and need to be saved, typically by white folks with professional and academic credentials, many of whom have not studied or aren't familiar with the history and culture of the people they serve and are not immersed in that history and culture.

Solution-wise, one big piece of the solution is to invest in black institutions and organizations that can do the work of helping to repair the damage that's been done to people of African descent.

Kevin Shird: Basically, there are already organizations on the ground like yourself doing the work in this city, and instead of creating new organizations, you're basically saying invest...in the groups that are already doing the work and are already successful at doing the work.

Dayvon Love: What the notion of black inferiority does is that it instructs people from the outside to see our people as objects of their thought experiments. They're like, "Oh, I know what will fix them." They try all these thought experiments that are more about their own conjecture, but not about their experience in the community.

I think, to your point, in terms of investing in people that are already in the community, one of the roadblocks is that there are particularly white-controlled, white-dominated nonprofit institutions and institutions in general that are put forward given the social capital to be seen as the leading advocates on a particular issue.

What you have is the people who are making policies for our communities being people who are external to our communities, and in fact are exploiting the problems in our communities. There are people that make six-figure salaries to prescribe solutions that get them access to capital that aren't about fixing our problems, but about making their organizations sustainable so that they can continue to get funding and make the salaries that they make. That's a really painful thing for a lot of people.

I think in Baltimore they're coming to grips with it, because there's essentially an industry buttressed on black misery and suffering. If we were to upend that industry, there are a lot of people who would lose jobs, because I guess the point that I'm making is that there is a huge financial, economic incentive for the institutions as they exist, to stay the same.

Kevin Shird: Almost like a nonprofit-industrial complex in place.

Dayvon Love: Exactly. Exactly.

Kevin Shird: Yeah. How did we get here? Give us a little bit of history. How did Baltimore get in this situation? Early on in this book I wrote a chapter on 1968. I looked at the history of that era and a lot of the similarities to today, and it was scary, because you're talking roughly fifty years later. Fifty years later, how did we get here? How did we get to this situation?

Dayvon Love: I think one of the biggest things for people to understand—and a lot of people don't understand—is the importance of integration and how integration really was the beginning of the end of the development and cultivation of black institutions.

What happened was, pre-integration, many of the functions that government now does for the community were done by community-based organizations: churches, civic institutions, the like.

When integration happened, you now have government intervening into the affairs of the black community, whereas before integration, white folks didn't care. We had to do for ourselves, and build an ecology of institutions that were mutually reinforcing in order to sustain ourselves.

When integration happens, you have individual black folks that have been able to ascend to positions of leadership and power so that they can personally benefit. What this does is this takes away resources. It takes away an infrastructure from black institutions, because now all that social and economic capital is leaving our communities, now going into white communities.

What you have is black folks taking the social and economic capital that came from our ranks and investing to fortify the institutional power of white institutions to make decisions about black people.

What we have today is a situation where, again, an industry of folks making decisions about the lives of black folks, expanding the institutional capacity of white folks and the white collective mainstream to make decisions about black folks.

If we just look through our history, when people have the power to govern the institutions that affect their lives, they do better.

This isn't to say go back to segregation. This is to say it's important to build the institutions so that we're making decisions about the institutions that govern our lives. If we just try to integrate ourselves to the mainstream, we're only going to get a few individuals into those mainstream institutions. That's not going to cultivate the collective success of our community. I think we need to start thinking collectively about building institutions specifically for black people so that we can collectively advance as a community instead of just individual people.

Kevin Shird: You spend a lot of time in Annapolis talking to decision-makers, talking to legislatures. In your view, where's our black community leadership now? Why aren't they on the same page as us? Everything you're saying makes a lot of sense to me. Why aren't we on the same page with our leadership?

Dayvon Love: I think there are only two reasons. One is the willful lack of understanding of our history and culture from our people. There are a lot of our folks, black folks, who don't have a solid grounding in the history and culture. Because of the ways in which images and representations of black folks have circulated as being highly criminal, as being pathological, it undermines our self-concept. It undermines our ability to be proud of ourselves, so there are many black folks who attempt to capitulate to the social mores of white folks, to want to be accepted, to want to be liked.

The best way I've heard it explained, Dr. John Herbert Clark, talks about this concept of ego starvation, this idea that black folks have been beaten down so bad that anything, any opportunity being close proximity to something important that makes us feel like a big deal, we gravitate toward. I think what that has done is incentivized our leadership to sell out for pennies, to sell out for real cheap. What happens is people confuse an individual person getting into a position of leadership within white institutions with collective black empowerment. Again, that just goes with a lack of pride and understanding about the importance of black collective empowerment. That's one reason in terms of black leadership.

The second reason that I think our black leadership is ineffective is because we have not effectively organized the institutions in our community as a machine behind our leadership.

I'm not often a defender of black leadership as it currently exists because much of it has been very lackluster. What a lot of black elected officials are left with is being appendages of white corporate institutions.

There isn't an organization based in our community that will give them the tools they need to be able to effectively navigate the terrain. For instance, let's say you have a legislator that's really big on second amendment stuff. They have an entire machine behind them of people who phone bank, of people who will show up to Annapolis, of people who will send out mass communications. We need that kind of machine here in Baltimore that is owned, controlled collectively by black folks, so that we can have the ability to then provide cover for the elected officials who are in office.

Now I do think, as a person who's generally committed to empowerment of black folks, if you're an elected official, a part of your job is to help to try to organize that machine, to help do the things necessary to build the apparatus in order to give you the cover you need. Unfortunately, a lot of our leadership isn't that committed to the idea of collective black empowerment to the extent that they will put the work in necessary to help facilitate the building of that kind of political machine.

Kevin Shird: When I was in East Baltimore the other day, I was thinking about the lack of access to basic needs, like food and supermarkets, right? And it dawned on me. How did we even get to a place like this? How is it allowed to happen? If we're looking at solutions, what would you like Baltimore to look like ten years from now?

Dayvon Love: There are a series of institutions that need to be built and owned collectively by the masses of our people in this city. Those things include the development of civic institutions that are specifically geared to and controlled by our community that address social issues.

Kevin Shird: When you say civic institutions, be a little bit more specific.

Dayvon Love: Institutions, for instance, that do political education. When I say political education, not just voting.

Kevin Shird: That's important stuff.

Dayvon Love: Yeah, but getting people to understand the process. A lot of people don't understand that Annapolis is the state capital where legislation is [adopted].

Kevin Shird: Right.

Dayvon Love: A lot of people don't know what the state controls, what the city controls. A lot of people don't understand the way money moves, the quasi-government institutions that money flows through. It's important to have civic institutions that we only control that are financed so we can do a lot of these civic kinds of activities. One of the things that we're doing, we got a contract to teach civics to elementary school students.

Kevin Shird: In Baltimore?

Dayvon Love: In Baltimore.

Kevin Shird: Wow.

Dayvon Love: Those are the kinds of things that we need to invest in, institutions that do that. We also need community-owned CDCs (community development corporations). One of the biggest problems of Baltimore is the way that development happens. In Baltimore, you have big developers that go through quasi-government institutions that are connected to political power. This is where you get a lot of the gentrification. If you have community development corporations from which investments are made in those institutions to plan communities, to build up communities and neighborhoods, then you don't have gentrification. You put money in the hands of people in that community to plan the kinds of things that exist in the neighborhoods, so you're not pushing people out of their communities.

Kevin Shird: Right.

Dayvon Love: What it also does is it creates a container so that they can engage in collective decision-making about things like education or criminal justice, because then they have the institutional wherewithal to pay people to go see what's happening inside the prisons or go see what's happening inside the schools, because of the nature of the institution.

I think the other thing, and this is something that's also down the road, is the development of independent credit unions collectively owned by black folks in the city. I think one of the things that we're faced with, is that in order for us to get the capital we need to do projects for our community, we have to go to institutions that don't have a vested interest in our community.

We need to develop financial institutions so that we can effectively circulate money and resources in our communities. You hear a lot of people talking about "buying black." That's good on an individual level, but the problem with that is that it relies on people making individual choices to do it. What a credit union would do is it would create a collective financial interest in everybody supporting each other. It takes a lot to build it, so that's definitely a longer term goal.

Those are the three things that I would say are necessary. The last thing is, and this is LBS on a long-term vision, LBS. Leaders of a Beautiful Struggle is part of our longer term vision to have a full-scale, world-class public policy apparatus, just like you have the Brookings Institute, the Manhattan Institute. We need a fully functioning public policy apparatus that focuses specifically on the issues of black people. Having that apparatus will help us be able to monitor what happens in the public policy arena, specifically for our communities.

Kevin Shird: In this vision, what do you see the role of the churches in Baltimore, because we have a lot of churches in Baltimore that have a lot of resources that are clearly being underutilized. Do you see a role that they could play in helping to bring the city back together?

Dayvon Love: I think the operative word in that is "could." I think they could play a tremendous role. Historically, the black church has really been the hub for black freedom struggle in the western hemisphere. I think what has happened is that churches in many contexts, particularly the big mega-churches, have become gatekeepers in ways that have undermined, again, collective black political power. Individual pastors get access, their churches get access to city hall. You have a city hall relationship to get into certain meetings, to certain resources, but at the expense of building independent black political power. One thing I want to say about that is that I think a lot of times we're quick to jump on short-term solutions and fixes. Support the Democrats so that you can get a couple of trinkets here and there.

People a lot of times don't want to hear the concept of letting us begin to build our own political infrastructure so we're not relying on the Democrats. That's not going to yield benefits right away, but it's one of those things that once you build an independent apparatus, then when you're negotiating with the democrats, you're negotiating from a position of strength, not from a position of needing to be dependent on them for our interests in the political arena.

We need to have our own power I think the churches could play a role for at least beginning to finance some of the development of that infrastructure. They would have to give up the gatekeeper function. They would have to give up their access in order to be a part of building that, again, that black collective political infrastructure that could help to be the engine for collective empowerment.

Kevin Shird: Do you foresee in Baltimore an opportunity for another Freddie Gray type incident? Do you foresee that arising again in Baltimore?

Dayvon Love: It really depends. My theory—and there's a sister name Stacy Patten, who used to be a writer for the Sun. She's a scholar. When she came to Baltimore, I asked her about what she thought about this theory I'm about to describe and she concurred. Police brutality has been an issue for decades. My theory is that when Trayvon Martin was killed by George Zimmerman, it was a huge media spectacle. I remember people had to protest and fight just to get Zimmerman charged. There was a big media interest and it started off as a small story that snowballed into a bigger story. It then snowballed into an even bigger story. When it hit the national mainstream, I think corporate media realized they can get tremendous viewership from this theater of a police brutality case.

I think what began to happen was they realized we need to start covering more of these cases. Then we see the explosion of the coverage of police brutality.

Kevin Shird: It's been happening all across America.

Dayvon Love: Exactly.

Kevin Shird: In the black community, police brutality is nothing new to us.

Dayvon Love: Exactly. Exactly. You see the Jordan Davis, the death of Jordan Davis. You have Mike Brown, obviously. You have all these different examples that are now newsworthy. What happens in Baltimore is a snowball from what happens in Ferguson in a sense that Ferguson creates a media context, an appetite for those kinds of stories. When Freddie Gray was hospitalized, I was at an event at a church downtown. I got a text from a family member who was at the hospital. They sent me a picture, the picture people keep seeing on the news. Sent me a text with the picture. I remember looking at that picture and saying to myself, "OK. This is about to be my life for the next couple of months."

I had the sense that the media was going to create a context for this to explode. That, combined with people's frustration with the lack of progress on the issue of police brutality, really amplified everything. In terms of another uprising like that happening, if I have to guess, it is most likely to happen if the white police officers seen in the video, when Freddie Gray is taken into custody, if those officers don't go to jail, I can see folks being upset. I see that as probably being the biggest potential for an uprising that I can see in the immediate future.

Kevin Shird: You work with young people every day across Baltimore…so you have your finger on the pulse of the youth. How are the youth feeling today after the uprising, after one trial so far? How do they feel about this situation? Are they afraid just being in the streets? Are they afraid of becoming a statistic in that sense of police brutality? How do they feel?

Dayvon Love: I'll tell you something. Most of them do not care about the stuff that we think they care about. Young people are in a very precarious situation in this city in terms of finding gainful employment, in terms of feeling like they have opportunities. For them, police brutality, being harassed by police is like, whatever. That happens all the time to these kids. It's not like they're seeing this coverage and are more scared than they were before they saw it.

Kevin Shird: It's not new to them.

Dayvon Love: It's not new to them at all.

Kevin Shird: It's new to the media and the people on the outside.

Dayvon Love: Exactly.

Kevin Shird: It might be new to some class of America, but it's not new to the young black person living in Baltimore.

Dayvon Love: Right. All they care about is really trying to make a better life for themselves than the one they had yesterday. I think sometimes people lose sight of that. People lose focus on that. For us, the issue of police reform was one policy issue, but there are a bunch of other issues that we need to address to deal with…the problem holistically. I think young folks, they—

Kevin Shird: They're getting a sense that people care about it politically, but don't care about them.

Dayvon Love: Right.

Kevin Shird: They don't see a lot of these people who are out here doing a lot of this advocacy work.

Dayvon Love: A couple weeks ago, I went and spoke to a class of high school students at Forest Park, the school I graduated from. For me, just talking directly to them…there aren't a lot of folks who do the kind of work that I do who go talk directly to them, that relate, that have a lot of the same experiences. One of the things that I made sure I reiterated was that I genuinely care about figuring out ways to make the communities they live in a better place.

Kevin Shird: Right, that's what matters.

Dayvon Love: Exactly.

Kevin Shird: Someone's going to come and actually fix this. Make this a better school. Make this a better community. That's what they care about.

Dayvon Love: I was talking to some human-services friends of mine who were going to Washington, DC, and they do a lot of work with the federal government. The comment they made to me was that Baltimore has been Baltimore for the last several decades. Those friends were telling me that the issues in Baltimore didn't become a national issue until those issues were viewed by the rest of the world, until we made CNN, until we made MSNBC, until we made the cover of the Washington Post. We struggle with what's been going on in Baltimore for decades. People have died. People have gone to prison. People have been hopeless and marginalized for decades.

Kevin Shird: On your wish list of the number-one issue that you would like to see addressed in Baltimore after all that's gone on, what would be the number-one issue that you would like to address?

Davon Love: The biggest thing is just building economic power. That's crucial. I think all other issues in order to operationalize the solutions need the financial infrastructure to be able to do it, and we need the kinds of policies that lend itself to the ability to have access to the financial resources needed to do that.

Kevin Shird: In closing, is there anything you would like to say? Any last words you'd like to cover before we finish?

Dayvon Love: I think I hit it all. All I want to see is real progress.

CHAPTER 9
SOLUTIONS

Since every major problem deserves a solid and sustainable solution, what is the solution for Baltimore? How do we break the cycle of poverty for those who cannot move to a more affluent neighborhood? Baltimore is a blue-collar, hardworking town with a lot to offer the world, and the potential to be a world-class city. But first there's work to do and issues to address. This can't be just more of the same lip service from our leadership and elected officials. Baltimore needs action.

Given what we now know about how poverty, pain, and anger contributed to the unrest and riots in the city, what do we do now? How do we reduce poverty and reduce unemployment in a town where jobs have poured out of the city for years because of outsourcing and a growing number of low-income part-time jobs in today's "shared economy"? The economy is growing because of new opportunities for social connections made possible by technology like apps and mobile communications. But while new companies like Uber have created opportunities for freelance drivers, they still are low-paying jobs with no benefits.

Poverty contributes to impoverished schools and poor health, which help lock the cycle in place because a poor education guarantees low-wage jobs or no jobs, while poor health handicaps individuals to work at all. So how do we improve the education of those living at the bottom of the income gap? And how do we increase the financial literacy of the impoverished, so they better understand what to do with what money they have, and avoid such "services" like payday loans or other very high-interest loans. Loans like these can easily balloon to the point where the homeowner cannot pay the mortgage.

Here I suggest a few solutions, first drawing on suggested solutions from previous conversations in the book. Then, I'll describe solutions that I have suggested earlier, particularly how to help impoverished youths get a college education to obtain a better income. Getting this education is critical because a minimum wage job in a McDonald's restaurant will not lift a person out of poverty, but a college education will.

Cutting Down the Poverty Rate

It may sound outrageous at first glance, but one simple solution for cutting the poverty rate in half, proposed by economic scholars Matt Bruenig and Elizabeth Stoker, is to send every adult and child $3,000 a year, as they describe in an October 2013 *Atlantic* article: "How to Cut the Poverty Rate in Half (It's Easy)."[79] This is not some harebrained scheme, given the authors credentials. Bruenig writes on economics and politics on his website, www.mattbruenig.com, and for the Demos Policy

Show blog; Stoker is a Marshall Scholar at Cambridge University and her work has appeared in the *Los Angeles Review of Books* and *Salon*. So, this is an article by writers with solid credentials. Some think they're crazy but I thought them to be very rational.

The basic idea of their approach is to reduce poverty by giving the poor money so they are no longer poor. It's an economically feasible solution, though the main obstacle will be political resistance. As they explain, 46.5 million Americans, or 15 percent of the population, lived below the poverty line in 2012. In economic terms, collectively these impoverished Americans were $175 billion below the poverty line, which is only 1.08 percent of the country's gross domestic product (GDP) and a quarter of the country's $700 billion military budget. This is also the amount that the United States spends on Social Security disability benefits. So, they could easily give that $175 billion in three-thousand-dollar payments to poverty stricken Americans.

These writers also point out that the country has already engaged in both official and unofficial efforts to reduce poverty, so this giveaway would be nothing new. For example, they point to Social Security, which is the biggest factor in reducing poverty for the elderly, since benefit levels increased dramatically in the 1960s. Without these programs the poverty rate would be much higher. Plus, unofficially, there already are programs that aren't counted as income, but help the impoverished, like food stamps (through SNAP), Section 8 housing vouchers, the Earned Income Tax Credit, and the Child Tax Credit.

Even so, these programs don't go far enough, which is why the writers propose giving low income individuals $3,000 per person, which they characterize as "Social Security for all, not just the elderly." They further suggest that this would be an easy program to run, although it would require about $900 billion, or 5.6 percent, of the nation's GDP. But the United States can easily afford it. One of the writers' suggestions is raising taxes, first on the rich, who would pay more in taxes, while the lower-middle class and poor families would pay less. The federal government could also cut tax expenditures on homeowners, personal retirement accounts, capital gains exclusions at death, and exclusions on annuity investment returns, which they characterize as a submerged welfare state for the affluent and that cost billions of dollars a year. Additionally, they suggest the $700 billion military budget could be trimmed.

In support of their ideas, they point out that there are already movements in European Union and other European countries to provide a basic income for all citizens. Then, with a basic income guaranteed, workers might seek better wages and working conditions. So, the "give-away" would help "level the playing field for the bottom 99 percent." Or if the country wanted a "more modest, target approach," it could increase the funding for existing antipoverty programs, which are designed to make a difference.[80]

So, is such an approach feasible? I wondered. In theory it sounds like an ideal solution, although as Bruenig and Stoker point out, politics stands in the way. When they were writing this article, they found neither the Democrats or Republicans had any interest in their approach, even though technically it is quite feasible. But perhaps now, given the growing awareness of the problem of inequality, poverty, and the anger and upheavals in so many major cities, perhaps they'd consider this option. I certainly think it could work and I would like to see some bold policy changes.

Educating the Media So Their Reporting Is More Accurate and Less Sensational

Reining in the news media will also help, since they tend to sometimes present misleading images of the riots and the damage they caused, which has primarily harmed the lower-income communities. This was described by Paul Solman in an article and *PBS Newshour* series: "Racism, Riots and Economics: If History Is the Guide, Why Baltimore Won't Recover Soon."[81] The first of the series of articles was published on May 15, 2015, shortly after the riots.

As Solman notes, there were many more riots in the 1960s throughout the country, but they were less reported since there was no instant news reporting or cell phone cameras back then. Moreover, though the damage of these riots was worse, the damage was felt primarily by African Americans, since the riots reduced our incomes, reduced housing values, and often destroyed local amenities, like shops. Afterward, the efforts to repair the damage was insufficient to offset the damage caused. Yet the media has made it seem like the rioting is worse today. As Solman notes: "One thing that I've heard from people I've interviewed [and] experts is a measure of surprise at how little urban unrest there's been now compared to the 1960s, given growing inequality."[82]

But inequality between whites and blacks is less now than in those years, as noted by Boston University economics professor Robert Margo, the incoming president of the Economic History Association and a well-known scholar on race in America:

> [The perception of growing inequality today] is surprising, because if we look over the course of the full twentieth century, the dominant trend between African Americans and whites is one of narrowing inequality. Differences between blacks and whites in income, wealth, education were vastly larger a hundred years ago than they are today, and they've narrowed over time pretty persistently. Those differences have narrowed more slowly in recent years... but I don't think we will ever go back to the events that we saw in the '60s, where riots were very commonplace, because I do think that most people recognize that they're counterproductive in their effects.[83]

Moreover, Margo says that the amount of damage that was done, compared to a typical riot in the '60s, is not as much, but the key difference is "the amount of attention that's been paid to these events," resulting in more long lasting effects. As he writes:

> The physical damage isn't huge, but the media attention is enormous. And we don't have ways of extrapolating from the experience of the 1960s to the world today with that level of media attention, both in the professional media, and the social media...In the '60s there were hundreds of riots. And most of them were never reported in the national news. Ferguson, Missouri and Baltimore are on the world stage...And that affects people's perceptions

of these places well beyond the immediate environment of those cities…[In the '60s] the most severe riots happened in a relatively small number of places, but the occurrence of a riot was much more common. Today, these events are extremely uncommon, and they receive intense media scrutiny when they occur."[84]

In short, the media has played a large role in blowing up these situations, which also stigmatizes the city. This is not to deny the basic problems and anger that have led to these upheavals. But the media has exacerbated the situation, so we must rein in the media so they don't further inflame the situation. The media could help by bringing in more qualified voices to help explain what is going on in the community and why.

Helping Low-Income Families Move to Better Neighborhoods

We could find other ways to help low-income families move to better neighborhoods, if they wish to do so. As described in "The Importance of Place,"[85] by David Leonhardt, Amanda Cox, and Claire Cain Miller discussing a study that looked at the earning records of millions of families with children that moved, and the results corroborated those of other studies showing that when poor families move to more affluent areas, their children are more successful than those who stayed in the impoverished communities.

This research again demonstrates the importance of the environment and it backs up the feelings in Baltimore that led to the recent protests, since children, especially boys, in Baltimore face the worst odds of escaping poverty.

When I dug deeper into the research, I saw the powerful positive effects that can occur for kids when families moved out of poverty. As noted by Raj Chetty, who conducted the main study on the effects of moving with Nathaniel Hendren, both Harvard economists, "Every extra year of childhood spent in a better neighborhood seems to matter."

Chetty and Hendren also found that the places with large African-American populations, both black and white children had longer odds of reaching the middle class and both benefited from moving to better neighborhoods. By contrast, certain large cities—including San Francisco, San Diego, Salt Lake City, Las Vegas, and Providence—were most conducive to upward mobility, and so were major suburban counties, like Fairfax, Virginia; Bergen, New Jersey; Worcester, Massachusetts; and Contra Costa, California.

What made these places better? According to Chetty and Hendren, "they have elementary schools with higher test scores, a higher share of two-parent families, greater levels of involvement in civic and religious groups, and more residential integration of affluent, middle-class and poor families."

So, it seems clear: Helping families move away from impoverished areas helps. The research has shown that the younger the children are when they move, the better, and these improvements continue into their adult life.

Improving Education in Schools

Another good strategy for reducing poverty is improving the education available to children and teens in Baltimore. One way to do this is by implementing Common Core standards, which prepare elementary school students for college, as John O'Conner describes in "Core Questions: How Does Common Core Address Poverty?"[86]

It is important to start early with this curriculum so students get the foundational skills needed to advance, and so they develop a love for learning early. The advantage of the Common Core is that it allows "districts across the United States to share tips, techniques and lessons that work best for low-income or minority students."

While Baltimore schools use the Common Core, more must be done to get students to meet those standards. Improving teaching incentives to get better teachers might help. So might outreach to parents to get them involved in and committed to their children's education.

Besides adopting the standards, it is important to implement them effectively, so children can better learn what they need to know to succeed in life. It is important for children to prepare for college and to want to go, so they are on track to make better incomes in the future, which will help them and their families rise out of poverty.

Then, too, it will help to involve the local community in the school, since community participation contributes to student learning. A good example of how this works is the Wolfe Street

Academy, an elementary school in southeast Baltimore. Valerie Strauss discusses this in her article, "Teacher Tells Congress: 'We Simply Cannot Ignore the Stunning Impact of Income Inequality and High Child Poverty.'"[87] Wolfe Street Academy has the highest percentage of Hispanic students in the city at 78 percent, with the remaining 22 percent evenly split between African-America and white students. While the school isn't in a high poverty area, much can be learned from its success. Over nine years, the school went from the seventy-seventh most successful elementary school in Baltimore, as measured by the Maryland School Assessment, to the fourteen during the 2013–2014 school year. Very promising progress, to say the least.

The reason for its success is the innovative community-school model, which provides various services and support for all students and families, so "academics can take center stage, students can achieve, families can thrive, cities can grow and our nation can flourish."[88] A community school site coordinator develops systems for teachers, administrators, students, and their families to help overcome any barriers to success. The result is that teachers have a better opportunity to teach and students have a better opportunity to learn. At the same time, parents have more trust in the school. Among other things, the site coordinator works closely with the administrators and teachers, and builds relationships with parents to learn what students and their families need. Then, the coordinator recruits the right community partners to meet those needs.

For example, the Wolfe Street Academy had twenty-four partnerships with community organizations that provide support and enriched learning opportunities for students. One of these is with the linguistic program at Johns Hopkins University. They help teachers learn about the students' native language and ethnic backgrounds so they can use that information to teach them.

Given the success of this model, we should spread this idea to more schools in Baltimore and throughout the nation.

Looking for Alternatives to Fight Crime

Still another imperative to combat poverty and inner city misery is to reduce the rate of arrests, especially during protests. Mayor Stephanie Rawlings-Blake has, in fact, tried to do this, and she stated this intention at a press conference where she said she would not combat crime by returning to the days of mass arrests for minor offenses—the policy when Governor Martin O'Malley was mayor.[89]

In support of this policy, the mayor's office showed a chart which indicated a steady decline in violent crime since 2006, when O'Malley left city hall and arrests were at their highest. Those days of high arrests in Baltimore were called the "bad old days" because so many people were locked up. It was also a time when "communities felt their kids were under siege," according to Rawlings-Blake, and she had no intention of returning to that tactic.

This effort to reduce arrests is a promising strategy, especially when combined with giving money to the impoverished, helping low-income families move to other communities, and improving education so kids have a better chance at success in life.

The Educate One Foundation

Finally, another solution might be the Educate One Foundation, which I'm planning to start soon in Baltimore to provide financial support to help underserved inner-city students go to college. I began researching the possibility following the days of the uprising in the city. During that time, I began to wonder if I had been doing enough personally in human services and philanthropy to be effective in the city. I began to wonder how I could do more to make a difference in the lives of young people in Baltimore who needed support the most. I had witnessed firsthand the pain in the eyes of the people during the marches and the protests in April and May. These were people who were sick and tired of being sick and tired, and they deserved better for themselves and their children. But seeing their pain made me think more about what I should and could be doing to help.

I began looking at breaking the cycle of poverty through higher education. I found that the need for more financial support was critical, as I spoke to African-American students in colleges across the country, particularly historically black colleges and universities, and found that many of these students had some very challenging financial burdens. With this in mind, I began to think about creating an Educational Scholarship Fund to support inner-city students bound for college.

I've proceeded to develop the Educate One Foundation, which would be a Baltimore-based 501(c)(3) nonprofit organization. The organization would provide financial support for the financial needs of low-income students seeking to further their education. Many students across the country face financial problems that prevent them from going to college, often forcing them to drop out or not attend at all. The EOF will provide financial resources to first-year college students to support them in the completion of their freshman year.

More specifically, my proposal for the EOF includes the following key points:

Financial Challenges

- Attending college requires a significant financial investment. Tuition and room and board comprise the bulk of the costs, but there are also costs associated with daily college life, including textbooks, furnishings for dorm rooms, traveling home on holidays and in case of emergencies, participating in on-campus activities, engaging in recreational activities, and in general being part of the campus community.

Educate One Foundation's Mission

- The mission of the Educate One Foundation is to provide financial assistance that will:

  (1) Increase participants' likelihood of staying in school

  (2) Eradicate systemic issues that affect underserved students

  (3) Break the cycle of poverty through education

Background

- The afflictions of poverty don't just disappear after a student gets into college. The gap in college graduation rates persists. According to a thirty-year study conducted by Johns Hopkins University of low-income children,[90] almost no child from a low-income family makes it through college. Of the children from low-income families, only 4 percent had a college degree at age twenty-eight, compared to 45 percent of the children from higher-income backgrounds. Low-income students who scored between 1200 and 1600 on their SATs were half as likely to finish college as their counterparts in the top 25 percent of the income distribution. Economic distress can dim a student's chances by forcing him or her to take on part-time jobs or reduce his or her credit load to help out at home.

Statistics

- In 2013, 89 percent of undergraduates at Morgan State University in Baltimore received Federal Pell grants, meaning they are in the highest category of need. For many, the socioeconomic barriers become insur mountable. The six-year-graduation rate is 31 percent. According to a White House report,91 "low-income students face barriers to college success at every stage of the education pipeline, from elementary school through post-secondary education, sometimes in spite of their academic achievements."

- Educate One Foundation will be a leading voice in the national conversation on breaking the cycle of poverty through education. The fund is designed to fill the gap for students who have academic achievement and desire to go to college, but not the means. Eligibility criteria for the scholarship recipients are:

(1) Baltimore residency

(2) A family income below the national poverty level

(3) School senior in a Baltimore high school

(4) GPA of 3.50 or higher and a minimum SAT score of 2100 (combined math essay and verbal score) or ACT score of 30

(5) Demonstration of leadership abilities through participation in community service or extracurriculars.

Benefits

The benefits of a supplemental college scholarship can last a lifetime. Recipients and the community will benefit immensely from the Educate One scholarship as it helps students rise above their upbringing in poverty and become citizens of the world, all while giving back to the community.

In my opinion no child in America should fail in life simply because they could not afford college. This should be a non-starter for all American children. We must provide more if we are going to expect more from our children.

"The cost of college education isn't getting cheaper," said President Barack Obama. "We need to support as many students as possible."

CHAPTER 10
CHAMPION OF CHANGE

As the uprising and unrest in Baltimore moved out of the everyday minds of America, I realized that important questions needed to be answered here in the city. People had the right to know how city officials planned to fix what was obviously broken. The citizens wanted answers and weren't going to rest until they were satisfied. One of the most important questions was: What can we do today to make sure this never happens again here in Baltimore? What can we do now so that citizens won't feel like the only way to express their unhappiness with their current situations is to erupt?

A Little Motivation Can Do Wonders

Changes in policy are an absolute must, but we also have to change the way we see ourselves, and accomplishing that might take some inspiration. On May 4 I participated in a final interview in Baltimore with CNN News anchor Carol Costello. Before the interview I was thinking intensely about Baltimore and where we could go from here. Then I realized that the youth had to be a top priority if we were going to make any long-term progress in the city. That is when I thought about the need for inspiration and motivation from an important source. Here are the highlights of that interview on May 4 around 9:35 a.m.

Kevin Shird: I have a message for our president. Please don't let the people of Baltimore feel abandoned like the people in New Orleans felt abandoned during Hurricane Katrina. We need President Obama to lift up the spirits of the people, to lift up the morale of the people. The young people need to see our president.

Carol Costello: I think that in some people's mind, if the president goes to Baltimore, it would appear that he's taking sides. How would you answer those people?

Kevin Shird: Yeah, taking the side of the people and the young people in Baltimore is what we need—to see President Obama come to West Baltimore. Young drug dealers and gang members need to see the president of the United States come to their neighborhood. It has the potential to change their whole lives.

Let me just tell you this one story really quick. In 2008 during the presidential election, this was my first time involved in any election in my entire life. To see a black man elected, I had tears in my eyes. It also changed my perception of the world and what's possible. These young people in West Baltimore, they need that same experience. There's a 50 percent unemployment rate in that area of the city. Fifty percent of the individuals in that community are on some type of public assistance. Two hundred businesses have been destroyed in Baltimore during the riots. Older senior citizens are struggling to get medication. We know the CVS pharmacy was burned, but other pharmacies in that area have been burned down as well.

We need President Obama in Baltimore. Perception is everything, so we don't want to feel like the people in New Orleans [did] during Hurricane Katrina. We know our president cares, but we have to see it, we have to feel it. This is a history-making moment, to see a black man rise to the top as the president of the United States. [It is also a history making moment] to see him come to your neighborhood and tell you: "You're going to be OK. I've got your back." The [people of Baltimore] need to hear that. They need to feel it.

Carol Costello: Well, we'll see if President Obama heeds your call.

I'm not completely sure why I asked the President to come to Baltimore, knowing it was a long shot. Nevertheless, I thought I would make the pitch. Wouldn't that be a great thing to see the president of the United States walking the streets of West Baltimore? Walking the streets of Pennsylvania and North Avenue. Wouldn't that be a great sight to see? I really did think that such a visit would lift the spirits of the people and maybe, just maybe, change the trajectory of their lives. Maybe this visit would give them the pull they needed to be great.

I received some criticism on Twitter and Facebook for my comments during the interview with CNN. Some people couldn't understand my request to have President Obama visit Baltimore and see some of the carnage here himself. Some thought it was outlandish for me to say such things. On the other hand, the text messages I received from some people who knew me personally understood my motivation. They shared my view that something was needed to uplift and inspire the masses here in Baltimore. They agreed that a shot of inspiration was desperately needed at the time.

Baltimore Mayor Won't Seek Reelection

It's Friday just after sunrise, and I'm up early, as usual. On this bright, beautiful morning, I'm home in Baltimore replying to emails and preparing for a productive day. At the moment, I'm trying to stay connected to the world, writing a few chapters of a manuscript I had been working on and having a bowl of oatmeal, all at the same time. It's just a few hours into my morning ritual when suddenly the bombshell drops.

A news flash runs across the television in my living room that Baltimore Mayor Stephanie Rawlings-Blake will not seek reelection. I was blown away. This announcement came as a shock to the city and the nation, since she once seemed to have a bright future in politics. Then, the upheavals in Baltimore after Freddie Gray's death changed it all. Ironically, her announcement came a day after the city announced a $6.4 million settlement with Freddie Gray's family.

After seeing this report on television I went online to read what the *Baltimore Sun* had to say about the surprising announcement. I felt a certain uneasiness reading the news, since, as the article described, her every move had drawn scrutiny since Gray's death. In the Mayor's statement, she said she wanted to take election politics out of the decisions she was making for the city because she wanted to "help the city recover from the riots and prepare for the trials of the six police officers accused in Gray's death." She felt the time she would need to spend on her campaign would take away from the work needed to resurrect Baltimore, so she told the press at her press conference: "I need to spend the remaining fifteen months of my term focused on the city's future and not on my own."

While I think the announcement was a good one to help the city heal, because her actions during the riots had been much debated, it was bittersweet, because she had planned a celebration in a few days to open her new campaign headquarters, and she spoke of her love of Baltimore. But now there would be no campaign.

Still, while her statement shook up the Democratic primary race, which for decades determined the city's mayor, Rawlings-Blake received many commendations for her good work as mayor, despite the problems she faced during the uprising. Radio host Clarence Mitchell IV, a former state lawmaker, said she should be recognized for her contributions to the city. He noted that she had come to the city in "a very difficult time and she was the steadying rudder for a very long time."

However, after the upheavals in April and the widespread criticism over her response to the unrest, many questioned whether she could win reelection. Moreover, she seemed to run into difficulties because of the settlement with Gray's family, which strained relations with the city's police union.

In any case, her decision to withdraw from the race shows how the impact of the uprising is still felt throughout Baltimore. It also underlines the urgency to solve the long-standing anger of the dispossessed that led to the unrest. These are issues and solutions which *Uprising in the City* is designed to address.

Now that Baltimore is very much in the news, the city is ideally positioned to become a champion of change and set a precedent for the nation to follow. It can take a proactive role in showing how Baltimore can heal itself, which is what many major cities in the United States need to do, because many of them have experienced similar issues. The problems in Baltimore aren't isolated to Baltimore.

Some examples of other cities recently in the news because of unrest include Detroit, Philadelphia, Cleveland, St. Louis, and Oakland. Smaller cities like Ferguson, Missouri, and places like Staten Island have similarly seen protests. The triggering incidents have varied, though a major spark has been unjust arrests and police shootings. But there are other sources of anger, like the evictions of long-time residents when a city is gentrifying, as in San Francisco, and the poor and homeless are pushed out or herded into concentration-like camps to get them out of the city or out of the sight of tourists and visitors.

An article in *Forbes* on "Why Baltimore Burned" by Dan Diamond[92] illustrates these underlying problems that triggered the uprising in Baltimore, but are present in other cities too. Likewise, if Baltimore helps show the way, this leadership can provide an inspiration and road map for other cities.

For example, Diamond first describes why Baltimore burned, which could be the same reasons that many other urban cities in America may erupt. As he writes, some of the reasons include the pent-up anger over police brutality and Gray's mysterious death, and the looters who robbed stores and beat up reporters in broad daylight. But beneath these expressions of anger, the real culprit is that "for decades, Baltimore has struggled to solve persistent inequality that puts people down—and keeps them down."

The result of this inequality is that life in Baltimore is a tale of two cities. While Diamond grew up in Charm City, which stretches along tree-lined streets near Johns Hopkins University, the art museum, and a half dozen private schools, Freddie Gray died in the other city. The city where a quarter of the residents live below the poverty line and the employment rate is 19 percent where the riots broke out. In this city, fewer than 60 percent of the high school students graduate—the worst percentage of graduates in the state. Diamond also cites the terrible health statistics for the poor in the city: black infants are nine times more likely to die before their first birthday than white infants, and AIDs cases are nearly five times more common in the black community than in other communities. While the wealthy and poor neighborhoods are only six miles apart, the average life expectancy is twenty years less for those who are poor.

I could go on and on with these statistics he cites, many of which I have described in chapter 5,[93] "Poverty and Pain." But the point is that this pattern is similar to the great divide between the haves and have-nots in other cities, though specific numbers might differ. And all of the other cities, like Baltimore, are in desperate need of solutions. For example, as Diamond points out, more than 35 percent of the residents in Cleveland live below the poverty line, as do more than 39 percent of the people in Detroit. The difference in unemployment rates in different parts of those cities, too, illuminates the problem. For instance, in Washington, DC, the unemployment rate in the impoverished part of the city is 16.5 percent, whereas it is only 5.4 percent in other areas.

Given these problems in multiple cities because of inequality, that's where Baltimore can take the lead in recognizing what fixes are needed and making these fixes, like a beacon showing other cities what to do. Essentially, we need to fix broken schools, create opportunities where no opportunities exist, and provide training so people can move on to better jobs.

In short, we need to come up with a plan for what these fixes should be and how to implement them. And beyond fixing Baltimore, we need to take action to inspire other cities to create their own action plans. What happens in Baltimore can, in this way, serve as a model for other cities: it can become a champion of change.

Rebuilding Our Economic Image

According to a *Fortune* article, "Baltimore, Tarnished by Riots, Tries to Rebuild Its Economic Image," in the wake of the unrest provoked by Freddie Gray's death, Baltimore's elected officials and small businesses are pulling together to give the city's reputation a makeover.

As the article describes, Baltimore couldn't ask for a better salesman than Robert Wallace. The CEO of the energy engineering and technical services consulting firm Bithenergy, Wallace grew up in the city and attended Baltimore Polytechnic Institute, a public high school, before he enrolled in the University of Pennsylvania and later Dartmouth. Since then, he has launched three companies in the city, including Bithenergy.

But since protests in April, he's run into a bit of trouble with his pitch since Bithenergy's headquarters are in the direct path of the protestors, even though it was left untouched. However, as Wallace told *Fortune*, after that he had trouble recruiting new talent. "If I had an opening [before the protests] and I interviewed ten people I may have had three or four interested in taking the job," but afterward he only had one or two.

Even so, the company has been thriving nationally. It has installed and maintained more than twenty solar energy systems with more than thirty-three megawatts of solar energy in Maryland, Virginia, Massachusetts, and Pennsylvania. And it is rated number one on Fortune's 2015 Inner City 100 List, a ranking of the fastest-growing companies in urban areas by the Initiative for a Competitive Inner City. In 2014, its revenues were over $7.2 million and it had a five-year growth rate of nearly 3000 percent. In fact, it is one of four Baltimore-based companies on this year's list. The others are the brand agency Planit, the events company P. W. Feats, and the web-development firm SmartLogic.

Following such a high-profile incident, you'd expect job hunters to be wary of Baltimore, as Wallace describes. But William Cole, president and CEO of the Baltimore Development Corporation, insists that when the city as a whole is considered, the "exact opposite" has been the case. The city has received "more inquiries from companies interested in growing or relocating here," and major construction projects are "moving faster now than they were before." Perhaps the decline of interest in Bithenergy says more about a declining interest in solar power than about Baltimore's potential to attract new companies and jobs.

The city does have an appeal for new companies which seems to be the case, since before and after the Freddie Gray protests, several notable companies have moved to Baltimore or struck deals indicating their desire to stay. Danish jeweler Pandora moved its headquarters, along with 250 employees, to the city from the nearby suburb of Columbia, MD, early this year. Under Armour CEO Kevin Plank, whose company is based in Baltimore, has snapped up real estate around the city, including a recent deal for forty-three acres of waterfront property in the city's Westport neighborhood. Under Armour plans to build a new world class headquarters there. In March, Amazon opened a one-million square-foot distribution center at the site of a former General Motors plant that closed in 2005, in part in response to the city and state's attractive terms. Together, they gave the e-commerce giant more than $43 million in tax incentives to lure the company, provided that Amazon to hire at least a thousand people. In July, Amazon more than complied with the deal, having already hired 2,500 employees.

Despite those flashy deals, the city is plagued by a high unemployment rate. It was 8 percent in August, the most recent month data is available. That's 2.9 percentage points above the national average. Then, again, considering that the city's unemployment rate stood at 11.8 percent in August 2010, Baltimore has come a long way.

You cannot separate Baltimore's economic problems from the mounting social challenges many of its residents' face. "We still continue to struggle with the chronic problems we've had for decades—drugs and a [high] crime rate," Cole says. The city reported 211 homicides in 2014, twenty-four fewer than the previous year's total of 235, which had been a four-year high.

Some of the city's local employers are trying to address these factors on their own. Johns Hopkins is the city's largest employer and was criticized during the protests for not serving all of Baltimore. But Johns Hopkins is trying to change that. In September, Johns Hopkins University and the Johns Hopkins Health System launched a program to address the city's economic divisions by hiring local companies for its design, vendor, and construction contracts and by committing to hire at least sixty employees per year from Baltimore zip codes with high joblessness or poverty rates. The institution is also participating in a program called Live Where You Work, which provides employees with grants of up to $36,000 to buy homes in the city and is intended to build a demand for more small businesses—restaurants, drug stores, dry cleaners—within Baltimore borders.

Baltimore's city government has also tried to encourage employment with incentive programs like the one it offered Amazon. In the wake of the protests, Baltimore's Small Business Administration announced that it would make a million dollars available in loans to help businesses that had suffered physical damage during the riots and to strengthen the city's small business community overall.

In May, Baltimore Mayor Stephanie Rawlings-Blake launched a campaign called One Baltimore, a coalition of business, non-profit, and religious leaders to address the problems that the protests laid bare. Wallace of Bithenergy is a member of the group and this past summer, he participated in an initiative to encourage local businesses to hire students from Baltimore's high schools as interns. He has typically hired two or three interns for paid summer positions, and this year he hired five, reflecting his philosophy of involving young people in the city's growth. As he stated:

> Businesses like ours are so critical to the survival of an urban center. If we can expose these young people to potential opportunities, it connects the dots between the choices they make today and their quality of life down the road. If we can connect those dots, they'll make better choices and be much better off.

A Conversation about Fixing America's Urban Problems

After researching the future of Baltimore, I decided to meet with author and producer Wes Moore for lunch in Harbor East to discuss the uprising from his prospective. The place is immaculate and the fact that it looks out onto the bright city landscape is always a plus. We were now in the Baltimore that many know well, but others don't know at all. It was like being in a bubble far from the warzone that we call Sandtown-Winchester, where people die and get high.

As we ate, our conversation turned to the fallout from the upheavals in Baltimore and what we could do to make the needed fixes both in Baltimore and elsewhere around the country.

So I asked Wes the question, "What do we do to make sure this eruption in Baltimore doesn't happen to the rest of the country?" And then I asked him, "How do we fix Baltimore and fix America at the same time?"

Wes and I have been friends for several years now. He always has a unique prospective on the world, but particularly on Baltimore. Wes was born and raised here and loves the city like his own child. He's the founder and CEO of BridgeEdU and runs a platform. His organization works with colleges and universities and community colleges. They do a substantial amount of work with Historical Black Colleges and Universities. They help students who are at a higher risk of not matriculating and finishing college and work to reinvent how college works for them so that they can get the momentum they need to compete and complete college.

Kevin Shird:	Wes, where is your organization based?
Wes Moore:	In Baltimore. Baltimore-founded, Baltimore-based.
Kevin:	I'm going to just dive into this conversation really quick. We know we definitely want to cover some important issues. So, when the uprising in Baltimore first occurred, in April, what were your initial thoughts?
Wes:	Well, I feel like the uprising wasn't just one day. I felt like we felt this growing for a long time. I was here in the city. I was home....As you watched the temperature getting hotter and hotter and hotter it was weird. It's kind of like the frog that sits in the pot, where the frog is fine in the pot when the frog's first in there. But as the heat under the water builds up—It's not until the water's boiling that the frog actually feels the heat.

I remember the sense of fear that everybody in Baltimore felt, simply because it wasn't about what was happening in that individual area. No one felt safe, I don't care what area of Baltimore you were in. It was also a feeling of disappointment and heartbreak. The fact that we let things get to this level, that we had allowed the frustration to build to a point when—I remember I was speaking with some people and they felt that we had no control over anything. I think that's what really made people so heartbroken. We should not have been surprised by the level of heartbreak that people felt.

Kevin: So, physically, you were in the city? When you first heard the news, what was your reaction?

Wes: You know, it's funny, because when I first heard what was going on—The very first time I heard what was going on, I got a call from the NBC network, because I do work with NBC, and they said, "Can you get to a studio?"

Kevin: Wow.

Wes: I said, "Why?" They're like, "Do you see what's going on in Baltimore?" I knew it was Freddie Gray's funeral on that day, but I had not heard about what was going on, yet, around the Mondawmin Mall area.

Kevin: So, this was on Monday?

Wes: That was on Monday. That's when I said oh no. Then I started making calls and I was like, wow. Then I got to the television and I was like wow. It's on and you could see how the police really didn't have a level of control as to what was going on.

It was a feeling of—you just weren't sure what the next steps were going to be. Usually, when these things pop up...you usually watch—it gets quelled very quickly. Police are trained to kind of put a clamp on things. You saw that was just not happening.

Kevin: Did you talk to your family—I'm quite sure you did—within that period? What was their feeling?

Wes: They were just hearing aboutwhat was going on. I was in a meeting and I first wanted to make sure they were safe. That's a mile and half from where I live, so I wanted to first call and make sure everybody's good. Everybody's good. OK. Now, what is the next step? That's when I realized I've got to go, so I took off from there. That's when we got together with the family to figure everything out and make certain that they were safe.

Kevin: How did we get here to this situation where, in 2015, we're having a riot or uprising in Baltimore? However we decide to title the incident, how did we get here?

Wes: Well, I think we got here because we've had decades and generations of folks who have not been heard. They don't understand why certain things are priority in certain areas of the city and certain things are completely ignored in other areas. We got here because of the level of disparity that we have on health, housing and education and all these other things. And policing. At some point, frustration builds up to a level that peaceful and quiet protest feels insufficient.

Kevin: You mentioned education. What role has education played regarding the issues in Baltimore?

Wes: I thought education was the great equalizer. Education was the thing that gives people a sense of hope and…a sense of aspiration, and makes people know that they can have a path to have something bigger. We have a situation, right now, where we have graduation rates in this city that are lower than anywhere else in the state. And people who do want to graduate from high school—two thirds of people who graduate from Baltimore city high schools, six years after finishing high school will have no higher education degree.

When you look at that and you understand the fact that, in 2020, eighty percent of jobs in Baltimore city will require some form of post-secondary credentials, we're then creating a society where you will have jobs available and the majority of your citizens won't be qualified for them. What does that mean to the future of your economy in this city?

Kevin: Where do we start with fixing that issue and making education the equalizer?

Wes: Well, first I think we need to start early. You need to get more people to understand the importance of early childhood education and are actually going to invest in it. It's funny, when people say, "Oh, we put three million dollars into this and it didn't work." It's like, "Yeah, because you actually needed thirty [million]." If you think about how it works in so many other communities, money is not an object when it comes to how will the kids be educated. We have to figure out better ways to allocate resources. I think we have to do a better job of getting families and communities involved. Education doesn't just begin when a kid walks in a school, but education begins when that kid is in the womb.

Oftentimes, I hear people blaming parents and I'm kind of like—for most parents, it's not that they don't care, it's that for most parents, they just don't know. We have to be able to work on the issue education from that angle as well. We then have to do a much better job of thinking of things like summer learning loss. We have to do a much better job of thinking about preparation for school. We have to do a much better job when it comes to higher education and make sure that higher education assets are available for all people.

Kevin: Right. Earlier on, when I asked you about the uprising and you said that it kind of looked like the police were trying to just figure it out at the time, right?

Wes: Just trying to control it.

Kevin: What are your thoughts on policing, not just policing in Baltimore, but policing across the country. We've had several incidents happen. I just want to hear your thoughts and how it related to that Monday evening at Mondawmin Mall.

Wes: Well, first the idea of unequal policing in Baltimore is not a new thing. It's not like from the Freddie Gray arrest we learned anything new, because I think for so many people in Baltimore, police brutality has been a long standing problem.

There were people who were shocked when they heard, "Oh, man, a kid got arrested and an hour later he's in a coma and a week later he's dead." But there were a lot of people in Baltimore kind of like, "OK, I've heard that story before." You know the story of Mike Brown. You know the story—these aren't new stories. I think people understand that disparity in policing does exist. I think people appreciate the fact that's it's not all policemen, but I think people also appreciate the fact that there is a culture that has to be fixed when it comes to policing and our communities. I think the other big thing is you saw what happened with the response. You then had a situation where everybody felt more tension. Citizens felt more tense. Police felt more tense. Everybody felt more tense. This wasn't something that just impacted one community. This is something that impacted all of us in every single way. People needed to understand that.

Kevin: Absolutely. Let's just talk about Baltimore in the grand scheme of things. We know Baltimore's been broken for a long time, on so many levels. We just discussed a few things like education, like policing, but in the grand scheme of things: solutions for Baltimore? I just want to hear your opinions on where do we start and where do we end to make Baltimore a better place?

Wes: I don't think there's a place we can end, because I think Baltimore, like all places in this country, are always going to be a work in progress. We're never going to be 100 percent perfect. The thing that I know is that…we're nowhere near, fixed right now. At least I'd like to get to the point where we're getting close. Right now, we're not even close. It's difficult to say where do you begin, because I don't think there's a single thing that's going to tip the scale. We've got a lot of issue we've got to work on.

There are massive health disparities. There are massive housing disparities. Massive transportation disparities. Massive policing disparities. I think an issue that is going to permeate everything and make everything difficult is education disparities, where you have so many kids who are finishing high school but still need developmental work in every course. Students are finishing high school and they're not prepared for work.

They're not prepared for college. So, what did we just sell these kids? What did they just go through?

That's why I think that education has got to be a core thing that we have to figure out, because one of the big things that I think we have to think about [is] wealth creation. It's not just jobs, it's wealth. Communities that have really seen huge growth, particularly in the African American community, are communities that had a distinct focus on wealth creation. Communities like Atlanta. Communities like Washington, DC, even places that kind of shimmy around the issue, these are places that made wealth creation among their population a core focus of the way they went about their business.

Kevin: Let's just talk about jobs for a second, because the unemployment rate in Baltimore, especially among the African-American community, is painful.

Wes: Fifty percent. One in two African American men you see in this city [is] unemployed.

Kevin: Right.

Wes: One in two. That doesn't include under-employment.

Kevin: Should people be surprised when we talk about one in two African Americans in Baltimore being unemployed and then see a high crime rate?

Wes:	They shouldn't be surprised. We've got a lot of work to do in this area.
Kevin:	Right? How are we supposed to move forward? How are we supposed to feed our kids when the jobs aren't available?
Wes:	Listen, people are gonna survive. People have to survive. If we aren't coming up with legal, sustainable, God-honoring ways for people to survive, they will come up with illegal, unsustainable, and non-God-honoring ways to support themselves. You have to create opportunities for people to develop their own destiny and to secure their own destiny.
Kevin:	So, why do our leaders feel surprised when things go bad? Why are they surprised that there's an uprising in Baltimore? Why are they surprised that the murder rate here is one of the highest per capita in the United States of America?
Wes:	The only people who are surprised are people who aren't paying attention, period. If you're surprised, that's on you.
Kevin:	Are our leaders really paying attention? Or is it that they just don't care?
Wes:	Well, I think they do care. I think people do. I give people the benefit of the doubt. I think that they care, but I think for a lot of people, they're just not sure what exactly to do or what exactly caring actually looks like. These problems are hard.

These problems have been around for decades and no one wants to take responsibility for them because they feel like it's not solely their fault and you can't argue that it is. The reality is that there's not one person that's responsible for this, not one group. There's not one generation that's responsible for it. This thing is generational, but the thing that I know is that we've gotten ourselves in a predicament that if we're not making long-term and sustainable change, then we're going to keep on repeating the same stuff.

Kevin: We're talking thirty years of Baltimore leading the nation—in the top five—in the murder rate in the country. We've led in heroin overdoses in the country and HIV rates per capita, in the African American community, in the country. When are we going to start trying to fix this mess? And I know that's a loaded question.

Wes: Yeah, I don't know…it's hard, because I don't know many people in Baltimore that have not been personally affected by this. I could probably count the number of people that have not been personally affected by this on two hands. I'm talking about whether it's that someone's been murdered or a victim of violence.

Kevin: You've had some amazing success over the years as an author and writer and you continue to come back to Baltimore. Why?

Wes: It's my home. It's the only place I've ever been on this planet. I've lived a lot of places on this planet. I've traveled to over seventy countries now. It's the only place that's ever felt like home. You can't understand me if you don't understand Baltimore and you can't understand Baltimore if you don't understand me. I'm going to spend my time and my energy trying to help a group, help a place. I feel that deeply about it. I feel that passionately about it, because you're right. We don't have to be here. We can leave. You and me, both, right? We can pick up any time we want. I think we've earned that. I also think there's no place we'd rather be.

Kevin: It's hard not to take it personal when you're talking about home and home is not the way you want it to be. We know we have the potential to be great. We look at other cities, like you mentioned— like Atlanta, like Washington, DC—that have grown and are now destinations for America. If you had a wish list, what is the one thing that we can do for Baltimore to become a destination for America, in the next ten years?

Wes: We have to deal with a couple big issues. We have to deal with the drug addiction issue, the education issue, and the wealth-creation issue. If we can deal with those three things, I think we can transform the direction of our city. If we cannot deal with those three issues, then I think we'll continue to have a difficult time.

Kevin: Great. Any final words before we end?

Wes: I think my final word is that I believe deeply in this city…and the reason I believe deeply in this city is I believe deeply in its people. Some of the best people I've ever met are Baltimoreans. I think that good, bad, or whatever, we're proud of who we are and we're proud to call ourselves Baltimoreans. That's never going to change.

What we have to do, we have to be unafraid of imagining our city as a great place. We have to be unafraid of imagining our city taking care of our children. We have to imagine our city being unafraid of making sure that opportunities are real for its people and imagine our city being a place that you can walk down the street and not be fearful. We have to do a better job of imagining who we are and where we want to go and not be afraid.

Kevin: Thanks a lot. I appreciate that brother. Now, let's eat!

After I left, I felt a vibe of optimism for Baltimore. I've been friends with Wes for a long time and he has always been a glass-half-full type of guy. He's always looking for the positive and that's what I appreciate about him.

But it was a feeling in the air of hope and faith in the future for my city that made me feel good. For those of us who had been on the front lines of the battle, we could finally see a finish line where prosperity was within reach. One could tell that people living in the city had experienced an awakening. They realized now that they have been robbed of the American dream for all and wanted what they felt was deserved: a better life.

Life is a Beach Chair

Later, I received a surprising call from my good friend Twin, who had been telling me for a long time that he wanted out of the dope game. I hadn't spoken to him in a while and usually it's a red flag when I don't hear from a guy who says he wants to leave the streets. It's not an encouraging sign. The last time we spoke, I had given him the telephone number of the guys at the workforce development program I knew very well in West Baltimore. I wasn't sure if he would follow up because I still didn't think he was fully committed. When you've been involved in the streets for so long, doing something different is a real challenge, hard to achieve for many. But sometimes life is like a beach chair and you're tanning in the sun.

"Thanks for hooking me up with your guy Moses at the Center for Urban Families," Twin told me. "That brother really took me under his wing and looked out for me. I've got to be honest man, when I first went there I wasn't sure what to think or what to do. It was hard but it opened my mind." It was encouraging to hear that Twin had actually made contact with the people who could help him turn things around.

I said, "That's where it starts, bro. Change is all about a mind-set. Change is all about you looking at your life and saying, 'I want something better.'"

"You're right, man," Twin responded. "You're right. It's just been so long where I just didn't give a fuck no more. I tried to do things differently in the past, but out of frustration, I gave up too quick."

"I get it, bro," I said. "I've been there plenty of times. But then I said to myself, 'Enough of this. Shit has to change,' but I couldn't do it on my own. I needed some help. We all need help. That's why I sent you over to my guy Moses."

"That brother is real, man. He helped me get a good job, but he helped me in a lot of other ways. He helped me understand that if I wanted something different out of life, it had to start with me. And I learned a lot over there, but that job-training shit they have was a little crazy at first. At first they had me wearing a suit and tie every day and talking like a white man."

We both laughed at that, and then I told Twin: "Well, guess what? Your ass got a job and that's all that counts, right?"

"You're right, man," Twin said. "I'm just bullshitting, but I just want to say thank you, bro. This job saved my life. Shit got me off those damn streets. At the end of the day, all I want to do is take care of my kids, bro. You know how it is, man. All this motherfucker wanted is a chance man. That's it."

"Sometimes you have to give yourself a chance," I said. "Sometimes you have to create an opportunity for yourself, and I ain't talking about no street shit. I'm talking about wanting success so bad that you're willing to come out of your comfort zone and do something different, something you have never done in the past. That's where real change starts. So, where are you at now?"

"I'm at work until seven. I'm at the Marriott downtown working in maintenance."

"Well, you better get off the damn phone, before you lose the new job you just got!"

After we both laughed again, Twin continued: "This is all I wanted, Kev. All I wanted was a chance. I didn't want to die in the streets selling dope and hustling. After the riots, I thought that was it for me and for Baltimore. Life is crazy, man!"

"A lot of people thought that was it. A lot of people thought that was it for Baltimore, but they were wrong. It's never over until it's really over."

After we hung up the phone, I thought how Twin's story reflected the new hope for Baltimore. Twin got another chance to do something with his life, and that's all he wanted. The potential was always there, he just needed someone to help pull it out of him.

Now Baltimore needs another chance, another chance to be great in the world.

Although there are tremendous challenges in the city, there's an abundance of potential here in Baltimore. Even with all our faults and all of our issues, the people who live in Baltimore love this city. We love the crab cakes and the Baltimore Ravens and our Orioles. We love our house music and our barbershops. We love our art galleries and our Edgar Allen Poe history. From the projects of Poe Homes to the green gardens in Charles Village,

Baltimoreans love Baltimore. The changes we need to make are well documented. They aren't secrets anymore; we know what we need to move forward. A lot of hard work—and a lot of love.

(ENDNOTES)

1   *Baltimore Eclipse, The.* https://baltimoreeclipse.wordpress.com/2015/05/10/the-battle-of-mondawmin

2   McCabe, David. "Maryland governor glad Baltimore mayor 'finally' requested state aid," *The Hill,* April 27, 2015. http://thehill.com/blogs/blog-briefing-room/news/240264-baltimore-mayor-requested-states-assistance

3   Reutter, Mark. "Mayor takes a swipe at Hogan's inexperience, defends the timing of her request for troops," *Baltimore Brew,* April 29, 2015.

4   4. Ibid.

5   Chuck, Elizabeth and M. Alex Johnson, "Baltimore Mayor Stephanie Rawlings-Blake Under Fire For 'Space' to Destroy Comment," *NBC News,* April 25, 2015.

6   Neyfakh, Leon. "The Riots of '68: What the violence in the wake of the King assassination can, and can't, teach US about Baltimore today," *Slate,* April 27, 2015.

7   Schoen, John W., CNBC, Amber Payne, Erin McClam,
     and NBC News. "Baltimore Riots: Violence Scarred a City
     Dealing with Decline for Decades," *NBC News*, April 28,
     2015..

8   Neyfakh, Leon. "The Riots of '68: What the violence in
     the wake of the King assassination can, and can't, teach US
     about Baltimore today," *Slate*, April 27, 2015.

9   Covert, Bryce. "The Economic Devastation Fueling the
     Anger In Baltimore," *Think Progress*, April 25, 2015.

10   Keller, Michael, E. Tammy Kim, Tom Kutsch & Lam
     Thuy Vo. "Baltimore: The divided city where Freddie Gray
     lived and died," *Al Jazeera America*, April 29, 2015.

11   Schoen, John W., CNBC, Amber Payne, Erin Mcclam,
     and NBC News. "Baltimore Riots: Violence Scarred a City
     Dealing with Decline for Decades," *NBC News*, April 28,
     2015.

12   Rosen, Jill. "Study: Children's Life Trajectories Largely
     Determined by Family They Are Born into," *Johns Hopkins
     Magazine*, Winter 2014.

13   Ostrander, Madeline. "What Poverty Does to the Young
     Brain," *New Yorker*, June 4, 2015.

14 "Focus On Epilepsy," *Nature Neuroscience*, 18, no. 3 (2015), 317–475.

15 Op Cit., Jill Rosen

16 "Quick Facts," *US Census Bureau.*

17 Gray, Sarah. "6 Shocking Facts About Poverty in Baltimore," *ATTN*, April 28, 2015.

18 Ibid.

19 Koplowitz, Howard. "Baltimore Riots 2015: City Residents' Struggle Under Poverty, Income Inequality and Mass Incarceration Predates Freddie Gray Unrest," *International Business Times*, April 28, 2015.

20 Ibid.

21 "The Right Investment?: Corrections Spending in Baltimore City," *Prison Policy Initiative*, February 25, 2015.

22 Ellison, Charles D. "Baltimore's Slow Burn of Poverty and Hopelessness," *The Root*, April 29, 2015.

23 13. Ibid

24 14. Ibid.

25 Berube, Alan and Brad McDearman. "Good Fortune, Dire Poverty, and Inequality in Baltimore: An American Story," *Brookings*, May 11, 2015.

26 16. Ibid.

27 17. Ibid.

28 18. Ibid.

29 Badger, Emily. "How Baltimore and Cities Like It Hold Back Poor Black Children as They Grow Up," *The Washington Post*, May 6, 2015.

30 Ibid.

31 Sonenstein, Freya L. "Introducing the Well-Being of Adolescents in Vulnerable Environments Study: Methods and Findings," *The Journal of Adolescent Health* 55, no. 6, (2014).

32 Sonenstein, Freya L. "Introducing the Well-Being of Adolescents in Vulnerable Environments Study: Methods and Findings," *The Journal of Adolescent Health* 65, no. 5, (2013).

33 Sonenstein, Freya L. "Introducing the Well-Being of Adolescents in Vulnerable Environments Study: Methods

and Findings," *The Journal of Adolescent Health* 55, no. 6, (2014).

34 Ibid.

35 Ibid

36 Ibid.

37 MacDonald, Dwight. "Our Invisible Poor," *New Yorker,* January 19, 1963.

38 Galbraith, J. K. "The Affluent Society," *Houghton Mifflin Harcourt*, 1998.

39 Stone, Chad. "How to Deal with Globalization's Job Losses," *US News & World Report*, March 1, 2012.

40 Roberts, Paul Craig. "Globalization Creates Unemployment: American Job Loss Is Permanent," *Global Research*, October 28, 2010.

41 Ibid.

42 Renn, Aaron M. "How Globalization Isolates Struggling Cities," *GOVERNING,* January 2014.

43 Ibid.

44 Ibid.

45 Pethokoukis, James. "Don't blame globalization, China, or outsourcing for the Baltimore riots," *The Week*, April 29, 2015.

46 Drezner, Daniel W. "Globalization and Baltimore," *The Washington Post*, April 28, 2015.

47 Ibid.

48 Baker, Peter. "Obama Plans Broader Use of Clemency to Free Nonviolent Drug Offenders," *The New York Times*, July 3, 2015.

49 Badger, Emily. "How Baltimore and cities like it hold back poor black children as they grow up," *The Washington Post*, May 6, 2015.

50 Goldberg, Jonah. "To Break the Cycle of Poverty in Baltimore, Fix the Culture of Poverty," *TownHall Media*, May 6, 2015.

51 Puente, Mark "Sun Investigates: Some Baltimore police officers face repeated misconduct lawsuits," *The Baltimore Sun*, October 4, 2014.

52 Robinson, Eugene. "It's Time to Seriously Rethink 'Zero Tolerance' Policing," *The Washington Post*, May 4, 2015.

53 "Zero Tolerance" Debatewise, http://debatewise.org/
    debates/2595-zero-toerance/?action=history

54 Schwartzman, Paul and John Wagner. "As Baltimore
    Mayor, Critics Say, O'Malley's Police Tactics Sowed
    Distrust," *The Washington Post*, April 25, 2015.

55 DailyKoss and Illinifan17. "Listen to the People of
    Baltimore Talk About Martin O'Malley," Online video
    clip. *YouTube*, April 28, 2015.

56 "Urban Police—Policing Minority Citizens, Policing
    Juveniles, Policing Mentally Disordered Citizens, Policing
    the Homeless, Policing Crowds," *Yale University*, 2012.

57 "Micro-Policing Can Reduce Violence in Urban Hot
    Spots," *Institution for Social and Policy Studies, Yale
    University*, 2013.

58 *Introductory Handbook on Policing Urban Space*. New
    York: United Nations, 2011. https://www.unodc.org/pdf/
    criminal_justice/Introductory_Handbook_on_Policing_
    Urban_Space.pdf

59 Arias, Juan Sebastian. "Enhancing the Employment
    Chances for Formerly Incarcerated Americans," *Living
    Cities*. October 14, 2014.

60 Wascalus, Jacob. "Development Programs to Help Ex-Offenders Join the Workforce," *Federal Reserve Bank of Minneapolis*, October 1, 2013.

61 Ibid.

62 Arias, Juan Sebastian. "Enhancing the Employment Chances for Formerly Incarcerated Americans," *Living Cities*. October 14, 2014.

63 Ibid.

64 "Hennepin County Human Services and Public Health Department." MinnesotaHelp.Info. https://www.minnesotahelp.info/Providers/Hennepin_County_Human_Services_and_Public_Health_Department/Project_Connect/30?Returnurl= percent2fspecialtopics percent2fseniors percent2f20304 percent3f

65 "Careers." Rise, last modified 2016. http://www.rise.org/jobs/

66 Wascalus, Jacob. "Development Programs to Help Ex-Offenders Join the Workforce," *Federal Reserve Bank of Minneapolis*, October 1, 2013.

67 "SOAR Careers." SOAR, last modified 2016. http://www.soarcareers.org/

68 Wascalus, Jacob. "Development Programs to Help Ex-Offenders Join the Workforce," *Federal Reserve Bank of Minneapolis*, October 1, 2013.

69 Ibid.

70 "Fair Sentencing Act," ACLU, last modified 2016. https://www.aclu.org/node/17576.

71 "Governor Signs Historical California Fair Sentencing Act," ACLU, last modified 2014.

72 Anderson, Della. "It's Time for Smarter Sentencing," FCNL Staff Blog, last modified February 26, 2015.

73 Ibid.

74 Experience of Gini Graham-Scott with the Oakland Program.

75 "What is Community Policing?," *Discover Policing*, last modified 2016. http://discoverpolicing.org/whats_like/community-policing

76 "What Are Community-Based Crime Prevention Programs," *Bureau of Justice Assistance, U.S. Department of Justice*. Web. https://www.bja.gov/evaluation/program-crime-prevention/cbcp1.htm

77   Ibid.

78   Ibid.

79   Bruenig, Matt and Elizabeth Stoker, "How to Cut the Poverty Rate in Half (It's Easy)," *The Atlantic*, October 29, 2013.

80   Ibid.

81   Solman, Paul. "Racism, riots and economics: If history is the guide, why Baltimore won't recover soon," *PBS Newshour,* May 15, 2015.

82   Ibid.

83   Leonhardt, David, Amanda Cox and Claire Cain Miller. "An Atlas of Upward Mobility Shows Paths Out of Poverty," *The New York Times*, May 4, 2015.

84   Badger, Emily. "How Baltimore and cities like it hold back poor black children as they grow up," *The Washington Post*, May 6, 2015.

85   Leonhardt, David, Amanda Cox and Claire Cain Miller. "An Atlas of Upward Mobility Shows Paths Out of Poverty," *The New York Times*, May 4, 2015.

86 O'Connor, John. "Core Questions: How Does Common Core Address Poverty?", *WUSF Public Media*, February 10, 2014.

87 Strauss, "Valerie. "Teacher tells Congress: 'We simply cannot ignore the stunning impact of income inequality and high child poverty,'" *The Washington Post*, February 7, 2015.

88 Ibid.

89 Miller, Jayne. "Mayor vows not to return to days of mass arrests in Baltimore," *WBAL-TV 11*, September 26, 2013.

90 Rosen, Jill. "Study: Children's Life Trajectories Largely Determined by Family They Are Born Into," *The Hub, Johns Hopkins University*, June 2, 2014.

91 *Increasing College Opportunity for Low-Income Students.* Washington DC: The Executive Office of the President, 2014.

92 Diamond, Dan. "Why Baltimore Burned," *Forbes*, April 28, 2015.

ACKNOWLEDGEMENTS

Every morning that I wake up I realize that I have come a long way, but I also realize that I'm a work in progress. Personal growth only happens when you have people in your life who challenge you as well as show you the path forward. Thanks for showing me the path forward: Brooke Shird, Wes Moore, Joy Moore, Tia Gasgue, Moses Hammett, Joe Jones, Jenna Delgado, Antonio Delgado, Brenda Mills, Wanda Shird, Brandon Crawley, Zegory, Crawley, Karen Shird, Karl Shird, Charles Shird, Terrie M. Williams, Susan L. Taylor, Devin "Stuffy" Smith, Aaron Faulkner, Nina Keyes, David Simon, Steve Sobelman, J. Wyndal Gordon, Davon Love, Adam J. Jackson, Abdul Hakim Ali, Lucy Griffin, Wayne Cooper, James Worthy, Ryan Stewart, Kanika Feaster, Alex Gordon, Keon Evans, Jan Houbolt, Nina Keyes, Nicole Kirby, Guy and Nupur Flynn, Cynthia Todd, Jason Tagler, David Nevins, Shahid Malik, Bilal Ali, Glen and Sharon Middleton, David Warnock, Khayla Dorsey, Toni James, Jennell St. John, Anthony McCarthy, Derrick Purvey, Azikwe Deveaux, Ralph Moore, Charles Reynolds, Costella Denise Green, David Wilson, Reverend Frank Reid, Alvin C. Hathaway, Gini Graham-Scott, Natasha Victor, Nadir Nasheed, Linda Duggins, Al Granger, Gregory Kane, Maria Solis Belizaire, Latoya C. Smith and Sonja Sohn.